COSMIC DISCOVERIES

A GUIDE TO THE UNIVERSE FOR YOUNG EXPLORERS

SHREYASHI MANNA

To my fellow Astronomy enthusiasts,

And to my fellow friends and parents who believe in me.

Contents

Contents

Preface

Dear Young Readers,

I hope this message finds you filled with curiosity and a sense of wonder about the vast expanse of the universe. As I write these words, I can't help but feel a surge of excitement knowing that you are embarking on a cosmic journey alongside me. My name is Shreyashi Manna, and I am thrilled to introduce you to "Cosmic Discoveries: A Guide to the Universe for Young Explorers."

First and foremost, I want to express my gratitude to each and every one of you for picking up this book. Your interest in astronomy and your thirst for knowledge are truly remarkable. It is an honor to have you join me as we delve into the mysteries of the cosmos together.

Let me share a little bit about myself. I recently turned 18, and over the past two years, I have dedicated countless hours to crafting this book. As a fellow astronomy enthusiast, I understand the importance of having a resource that is both easy to understand and packed with fascinating information. That is precisely what I have aimed to achieve with "Cosmic Discoveries."

Throughout my journey of researching and curating the content, my goal has been to create a guide that will captivate and educate middle school and high school students like you. I have carefully selected the topics, organized them in a logical manner, and infused the text with engaging writing, fun facts, and lots of information in a fascinating and step by step manner.

Astronomy is a subject that holds endless possibilities for exploration, and I have done my best to cover a wide range of topics. From the wonders of our night sky to the secrets of our solar system, from the galaxies beyond to the mysteries of black holes, this book will take you on an extraordinary adventure through the cosmos.

I want to express my heartfelt thanks for embarking on this journey with me. Your curiosity and eagerness to learn are the driving force behind this book, and I hope that the pages ahead will ignite your imagination, deepen your understanding, and leave you in awe of the universe we call home.

Remember, this book is for you—the young explorers who are hungry for knowledge, eager to unravel the secrets of the stars, and passionate about all things astronomical. So, dive in, ask questions, and let your imagination soar. The universe is waiting to be discovered, and I am thrilled to be your guide.

Thank you for taking the time to explore "Cosmic Discoveries: A Guide to the Universe for Young Explorers." I truly hope you enjoy this cosmic adventure as much as I have enjoyed creating it. Together, let's embark on a journey that will forever change the way we see the world around us.

Wishing you clear skies and boundless curiosity,
Shreyashi Manna

Acknowledgements

I would like to extend my heartfelt thanks to my family, friends, and fellow astronomy enthusiasts for their unwavering support and belief in me. Your encouragement and enthusiasm have been instrumental in the creation of this book.

I am grateful to the educators and mentors who have guided me on this journey, sharing their knowledge and passion for astronomy. Your expertise and guidance have been invaluable.

To the researchers and scientists who have dedicated their lives to unraveling the mysteries of the universe, thank you for your groundbreaking contributions. You continue to inspire and push the boundaries of human understanding.

Lastly, I would like to express my gratitude to the readers who have chosen to embark on this astronomical adventure with me. Your curiosity and interest in the cosmos have been a constant source of motivation.

This book is dedicated to all the astronomy enthusiasts, friends, and family who have believed in me and shared my passion. Thank you for being a part of this incredible journey.

Keep exploring the stars!

Introduction: A Universe of Wonders

Welcome, young explorers, to the breathtaking journey that lies before you—a journey through the vast expanse of the universe, where stars twinkle, galaxies swirl, and mysteries abound. This book, *"Cosmic Discoveries: A Guide to the Universe for Young Explorers,"* is your ticket to an awe-inspiring adventure that will take you from the depths of space to the edges of our imagination.

As you hold this book in your hands, let me transport you to the night sky, where countless stars adorn the celestial canvas like shimmering diamonds. Look up and feel the immensity of the universe, stretching out before you, inviting you to explore its secrets. It is a universe filled with wonders beyond comprehension—a tapestry of light, energy, and cosmic phenomena waiting to be discovered.

But what is astronomy, you might wonder? Astronomy is the scientific study of celestial objects, such as stars, planets, galaxies, and everything else that fills the vastness of space. It is a journey of exploration and understanding, a quest to unravel the mysteries of the universe and comprehend our place within it.

For the past two years, I have embarked on a quest of my own—a quest to gather knowledge, uncover hidden truths, and present them to you in a way that is both accessible and captivating. In the pages that follow, you will find a curated collection of cosmic wonders, scientific insights, and mind-boggling discoveries.

This book is designed with you, the young explorer, in mind. It is a guide that will accompany you on your cosmic adventure, offering a wealth of information, vibrant illustrations, and engaging stories that will ignite your curiosity and expand your understanding of the universe.

But remember, this is not just a passive journey. It is an invitation for you to actively participate, to observe the night sky, to ask questions, and to seek your own cosmic discoveries. The universe is waiting to be explored, and you hold the power to unlock its secrets.

I would like to express my deepest gratitude to my fellow astronomy enthusiasts, whose shared passion has fueled the creation of this book. Your unwavering dedication to the stars has inspired me to delve deeper into the mysteries of the cosmos. To my dear friends and parents who have believed in me every step of the way, thank you for your endless support and encouragement.

Now, as we embark on this grand adventure together, let us turn the page and begin our exploration of the celestial wonders that await us. Prepare to be dazzled, inspired, and forever changed by the cosmic discoveries that lie ahead.

Welcome to "**Cosmic Discoveries: A Guide to the Universe for Young Explorers.**"

Let the journey begin!

CHAPTER TWO

Unveiling the Cosmic Tapestry

Introduction

Greetings, young explorers, and welcome to a journey that will ignite your curiosity and take you on an incredible adventure through the cosmos. In this book, "Cosmic Discoveries: A Guide to the Universe for Young Explorers," we will delve into the captivating world of astronomy—a field that allows us to unravel the secrets of the universe and explore the wonders that lie beyond our Earthly home. So, strap on your imagination and prepare for an exhilarating expedition filled with mind-blowing discoveries, fascinating facts, and a universe of awe-inspiring beauty.

What is Astronomy?

Let's start our cosmic exploration by understanding the essence of astronomy. Astronomy is the scientific study of celestial objects—everything that exists beyond our planet Earth. It encompasses a wide range of phenomena, from stars and galaxies to planets, moons, comets, asteroids, and so much more. Astronomers are like cosmic detectives, using their knowledge, tools, and boundless curiosity to unlock the mysteries of the universe.

Astronomy is an ancient discipline, as old as humanity's fascination with the night sky. Our ancestors, gazing up at the stars, developed myths and legends to explain the celestial phenomena they observed. But as time passed, humans began to seek more than just stories; they yearned to understand the nature of the universe itself. This quest led to the birth of modern astronomy—an endeavor that combines science, mathematics, and technology to unravel the secrets of the cosmos.

The Cosmic Playground

Imagine the universe as a vast playground, teeming with celestial wonders and mind-bending spectacles. Each object in this cosmic playground plays a unique role, like performers in a grand cosmic circus. Let's take a closer look at some of these dazzling cosmic performers:

1. Stars: Stars are like celestial fireworks, lighting up the night sky with their radiant brilliance. They come in all sizes, colors, and temperatures. Some stars burn fiercely like cosmic bonfires, while others shine with a serene and steady glow. Stars are born, they live their lives, and eventually, they reach their cosmic finale, sometimes exploding in a magnificent supernova. Stars are the building blocks of galaxies, and their stories are woven into the fabric of the universe.

2. Planets: Picture planets as celestial adventurers, each with its own personality and unique features. They orbit stars, just like our Earth orbits the Sun. Some planets are rocky like Earth, while others are gaseous giants, and a few are icy wonders. From scorching deserts to frigid worlds, planets captivate us with their diverse landscapes, dynamic atmospheres, and the possibility of harboring life.

3. Galaxies: Zoom out and behold the cosmic neighborhoods called galaxies. They are like cities of stars, billions of them, congregating together in a breathtaking display of cosmic artistry. Galaxies come in various shapes and sizes, from majestic spirals to fuzzy ellipticals. They dance and interact, sometimes colliding and merging, creating cosmic fireworks on a grand scale. Within these galaxies, supermassive black holes reside at their centers, pulling matter and distorting space-time itself.

4. Nebulas: Nebulas are cosmic canvases where stars are born and where stunning displays of vibrant colors dazzle our eyes. These celestial clouds of gas and dust serve as stellar nurseries, giving birth to new generations of stars. Some nebulae resemble glowing celestial dragons, while others take the shape of ethereal interstellar clouds. They remind us that the universe is not only a place of grandeur but also of breathtaking beauty.

5. *Cosmic Mysteries*: Among the wonders of the universe lie enigmatic phenomena that continue to challenge our understanding. Black holes, for instance, are cosmic beasts with gravitational forces so strong that nothing, not even light, can escape their clutches. Dark matter and dark energy, on the other hand, comprise the majority of the universe's mass and energy, yet their true nature remains elusive. These mysteries beckon us to explore and unravel the secrets that lie hidden in the depths of space.

Our Cosmic Toolkit

To navigate this vast cosmic playground, we need the right tools and instruments. Here are some of the tools that astronomers use to unlock the mysteries of the universe:

1. *Telescopes*: Telescopes are our windows to the cosmos, allowing us to peer deep into space and capture the faintest glimmers of light. From the humblest backyard telescope to colossal observatories, these instruments unveil the wonders of distant galaxies, reveal the intricate details of planets, and bring the farthest reaches of the universe within our grasp.

2. *Space Probes and Satellites*: To explore the more distant realms of our solar system and beyond, we rely on space probes and satellites. These intrepid travelers venture into the great unknown, sending back valuable data and images that expand our understanding of the universe. They have provided us with captivating images of planets, asteroids, comets, and even glimpses of other galaxies.

3. *Computers and Advanced Technology*: In our modern era, computers and advanced technology are invaluable companions in our astronomical pursuits. They allow us to analyze vast amounts of data, create detailed simulations of cosmic phenomena, and unravel complex mathematical equations that describe the workings of the universe. Technology empowers us to explore the cosmos in ways our ancestors could only dream of.

4. *Collaboration and Exploration*: Perhaps the most important tool in astronomy is collaboration. Astronomers from around the world work together, sharing knowledge, observations, and ideas to expand our collective understanding of the universe. They collaborate on projects, share data, and engage in conversations that push the boundaries of our knowledge. Together, they form a global community of cosmic explorers.

Embarking on Our Cosmic Journey

Now, dear young explorers, armed with this knowledge and equipped with our cosmic toolkit, we are ready to embark on a thrilling cosmic journey. Throughout this book, we will dive deeper into the realms of astronomy, unveiling cosmic discoveries that will leave you in awe. We will explore the planets of our solar system, delve into the mysteries of galaxies, witness the birth and death of stars, and ponder the mind-boggling concepts of space and time.

But remember, this journey is not just about learning facts and figures. It is about nurturing a sense of wonder, curiosity, and a deep appreciation for the beauty and vastness of the universe. It is about expanding our horizons and understanding our place in the cosmic tapestry.

In the next chapter, we will embark on our first expedition—a mesmerizing exploration of the night sky and its celestial wonders. Get ready to witness the dance of the stars, uncover hidden constellations, and unravel the stories written across the heavens in *"Chapter 3: Celestial Symphony: The Night Sky's Brilliant Orchestra."*

So, my fellow cosmic explorers, prepare yourselves for a journey beyond imagination. Let the cosmos be your guide, and let the stars be your inspiration as we embark on this extraordinary adventure together.

Until then, keep your eyes on the skies and your hearts open to the cosmic wonders that await!

CHAPTER THREE

Celestial Symphony: The Night Sky's Brilliant Orchestra

Introduction

Welcome back, young explorers, to another chapter of our cosmic journey. In the previous chapter, we learned about the vast playground of the universe and the tools we use to explore it. Now, it's time to turn our attention to the breathtaking beauty that awaits us in the night sky. Get ready to witness the celestial symphony—the captivating dance of the stars, the secret language of constellations, and the hidden treasures scattered across the velvet canvas of the cosmos.

The Night Sky: A Celestial Canvas

Look up on a clear, dark night, and what do you see? A tapestry of twinkling stars, shimmering planets, and a sprinkling of distant galaxies. The night sky is a mesmerizing canvas, displaying the wonders of the universe for all who dare to gaze upon it. But beyond its enchanting beauty lies a wealth of information waiting to be deciphered.

Stars: Celestial Fireworks

Let us begin our exploration with the stars—the celestial fireworks that illuminate our night sky. Stars are the building blocks of the universe, colossal balls of hot, glowing gas held together by gravity. From our vantage point on Earth, we see them as tiny points of light, but in reality, they are colossal spheres, some much larger and brighter than our Sun.

Stars come in a dazzling array of colors, sizes, and temperatures. They range from fiery blue giants to cool red dwarfs and everything in between. The color of a star indicates its temperature, with blue stars being the hottest and red stars the coolest. These luminous beacons are scattered throughout the cosmos, forming vast stellar communities known as galaxies.

Constellations: Mythical Patterns in the Sky

As we gaze at the stars, we can't help but notice the patterns they form. These patterns, known as constellations, have captivated humans for thousands of years. Early civilizations saw shapes in the stars and connected them with stories and myths, creating a celestial tapestry that tells tales of heroes, gods, and magical creatures.

Constellations serve as a celestial map, guiding us through the night sky. They help us navigate, find specific stars, and locate other celestial objects. The night sky is divided into 88 official constellations, each with its own unique story and significance. Some well-known constellations include Orion the Hunter, Ursa Major the Great Bear, and Scorpius the Scorpion.

Planets: The Wandering Stars

Amidst the backdrop of twinkling stars, we find the wandering stars—the planets. Unlike the fixed stars, planets move across the night sky, tracing their paths against the celestial sphere. These celestial nomads have fascinated humanity since ancient times, their movements tracked and studied by astronomers throughout history.

Our solar system is home to eight planets, each with its own distinct characteristics. Let's take a closer look at each of them:

1. Mercury: Mercury, the closest planet to the Sun, is a rocky world scorched by intense heat. Its surface is pockmarked with craters, remnants of countless impacts from space debris. Mercury has a thin atmosphere and experiences extreme temperature variations, swinging from scorching hot during the day to freezing cold at night.

2. Venus: Known as Earth's sister planet, Venus is shrouded in a thick atmosphere composed mainly of carbon dioxide. This dense atmosphere creates a runaway greenhouse effect, making Venus the hottest planet in our solar system. Its surface is a desolate landscape of volcanic plains, mountains, and deep canyons.

3. Earth: Our cherished home, Earth, is a haven for life. It boasts a diverse range of ecosystems, from lush rainforests to icy polar regions. The planet's atmosphere provides us with the air we breathe and shields us from the harshness of space. Earth's natural satellite, the Moon, orbits around it, tugging at the oceans and creating the ebb and flow of tides.

4. Mars: Known as the "Red Planet," Mars has long intrigued scientists with its potential for harboring life. Its rusty-red appearance is due to iron-rich minerals covering its surface. Mars has a thin atmosphere, cold temperatures, and a landscape dotted with ancient riverbeds, massive volcanoes, and vast deserts.

5. Jupiter: The largest planet in our solar system, Jupiter is a gas giant with awe-inspiring storms and swirling cloud bands. Its most iconic feature is the Great Red Spot, a massive storm that has been raging for centuries. Jupiter has a complex system of moons, including Ganymede, the largest moon in the solar system.

6. Saturn: Saturn, famous for its majestic rings, enthralls us with its beauty and mystery. These rings are made up of countless particles of ice and rock, creating a stunning spectacle. Saturn has many moons, including Titan, which has a thick atmosphere and rivers and lakes of liquid methane and ethane.

7. Uranus: Uranus lies on the outer fringes of our solar system and is classified as an ice giant. It has a unique feature—a tilted axis of rotation, causing it to appear to roll on its side as it orbits the Sun. Uranus has a cold atmosphere and a mysterious blue-green coloration.

8. Neptune: The farthest planet from the Sun, Neptune is also an ice giant. It is known for its vivid blue color, which is the result of methane in its atmosphere. Neptune has the strongest winds in the solar system and a moon named Triton, which is thought to be a captured object from the Kuiper Belt.

The Moon: Earth's Faithful Companion

In the grand celestial theater, there is one performer that steals the show—the Moon, our closest cosmic companion. The Moon is Earth's only natural satellite, a silvery beacon that illuminates the night sky and enchants us with its phases. It has been a source of inspiration and wonder for countless generations, fueling dreams of exploration and discovery.

As we observe the Moon, we witness its ever-changing appearance. From the dark shadows of the New Moon to the full glory of the Full Moon, the lunar phases captivate our imaginations. The Moon's surface, scarred by craters and dotted with mountains and valleys, reveals a tumultuous history of cosmic bombardment. In the future, we may even return to the Moon, establishing a lunar outpost and paving the way for further exploration of the solar system.

Beyond Our Solar System: The Milky Way and Beyond

Our cosmic journey takes us beyond the boundaries of our solar system, into the vast expanse of the Milky Way galaxy and beyond. The Milky Way, our home galaxy, is a massive spiral of stars, gas, and dust. It stretches over 100,000 light-years and contains billions of stars, including our own Sun.

But the Milky Way is just one among countless galaxies in the universe. These galaxies come in various shapes and sizes, from spiral galaxies like ours to elliptical and irregular galaxies. They form clusters and superclusters, congregating together in cosmic neighborhoods.

In our exploration of the cosmos, we have discovered that galaxies are not randomly scattered but are part of a larger cosmic web. This web is woven by invisible threads of dark matter, a mysterious substance that constitutes the majority of the universe's mass. Dark matter binds galaxies together, shaping the large-scale structure of the cosmos.

The Universe's Origins: Big Bang and Cosmic Evolution

As we ponder the vastness of the cosmos, we cannot help but wonder about its origins. How did the universe come to be? What forces shaped its evolution over billions of years?

According to the prevailing scientific theory, the universe began with an event known as the Big Bang. Around 13.8 billion years ago, the universe was a hot, dense singularity—a point of infinite density and temperature. Then, in an incomprehensible instant, it expanded, giving birth to space, time, matter, and energy.

Since the Big Bang, the universe has been expanding, cooling, and evolving. Galaxies formed, stars ignited, and planets took shape. Over vast cosmic timescales, elements like hydrogen and helium formed, paving the way for the birth of life. Today, astronomers study the early universe through the faint afterglow of the Big Bang—the cosmic microwave background radiation.

Conclusion

Congratulations, young explorers! You have now glimpsed the cosmic symphony—the mesmerizing beauty and profound mysteries of the night sky. From stars that dazzle our senses to the dance of planets and the splendor of constellations, the universe's celestial performers have enthralled humanity for ages.

In the next chapter, we will take a closer look at the life cycle of stars—the birth, evolution, and ultimate fate of these luminous cosmic beacons. Get ready to witness stellar nurseries, breathtaking supernovae, and the remnants left behind by dying stars in *"Chapter 4: Stellar Spectacle: The Life and Death of Stars."*

Remember to keep your eyes open to the wonders above, for the night sky is a limitless playground of discovery and inspiration. Until next time, fellow cosmic explorers, keep dreaming big and reach for the stars!

CHAPTER FOUR

Stellar Spectacle: The Life and Death of Stars

Introduction

Welcome back, young explorers, to another captivating chapter of our cosmic journey. In the previous chapters, we marveled at the beauty of the night sky, explored the wonders of our solar system, and delved into the origins of the universe. Now, it's time to turn our attention to the mesmerizing lives of the stars—the celestial beacons that light up the cosmos and shape the fabric of the universe. Get ready to witness stellar nurseries, breathtaking supernovae, and the remnants left behind by dying stars.

Stellar Nurseries: Where Stars Are Born

Our cosmic adventure begins in the heart of vast interstellar clouds, where stellar nurseries come to life. These regions, known as nebulae, are colossal cosmic cradles where new stars are born. Within the nebulae, dense pockets of gas and dust gather under the influence of gravity, slowly collapsing and forming protostars.

The interstellar medium, consisting of hydrogen, helium, and trace amounts of heavier elements, plays a crucial role in the formation of stars. Gravity acts as the sculptor, pulling together the gas and dust into ever-denser regions. As the density increases, the material heats up due to the release of gravitational potential energy. Eventually, a protostar is born—a nascent star in its early stages of formation.

As the protostars grow, they become hotter and denser, triggering nuclear fusion—the process that powers the stars. The immense gravitational pressure at their cores ignites a brilliant fusion reaction, where hydrogen atoms fuse together to form helium, releasing an incredible amount of energy in the process. And thus, a star is born.

The Birth of a Star: From Protostar to Main Sequence

Once a protostar has reached a state of equilibrium between its inward gravitational pull and the outward pressure generated by the fusion reactions, it enters the main sequence phase—the long and stable adulthood of a star. This phase is characterized by a delicate balance between gravity's pull and the energy released through fusion.

The main sequence stars come in a variety of sizes, masses, and colors. The most common type is the yellow dwarf, like our Sun. These stars shine steadily for billions of years, serving as beacons of light and warmth for their planetary systems. Other main sequence stars include massive blue giants, which burn brighter and hotter, and smaller, cooler red dwarfs.

The life span of a star on the main sequence is determined by its mass. Higher-mass stars burn through their fuel more quickly, leading to shorter main sequence lifetimes, while lower-mass stars have much longer lives. The main sequence phase is a period of stellar stability, where the star maintains a balance between gravity and radiation pressure.

Star Clusters: Stellar Communities

Stars rarely exist in isolation. They often congregate in stellar communities called star clusters. Star clusters come in two main types: open clusters and globular clusters. Open clusters are relatively young and loosely bound groups of stars. They contain a few hundred to a few thousand stars and are often found in the spiral arms of galaxies.

Open clusters are hotbeds of stellar activity. The stars within them are typically formed from the same parent molecular cloud and are therefore similar in age and composition. These clusters provide astronomers with an opportunity to study the effects of environment on stellar evolution, as well as the formation and evolution of planetary systems.

On the other hand, globular clusters are tightly packed groups of stars, consisting of hundreds of thousands or even millions of stars. These ancient cosmic cities are found in the outskirts of galaxies, forming a halo around the galactic center. The stars in globular clusters are much older than those in open clusters and provide valuable insights into the early stages of galaxy formation.

Globular clusters are like time capsules, preserving the characteristics of stars from the early universe. They are home to some of the oldest known stars, dating back billions of years. Studying these stars allows astronomers to unravel the mysteries of galactic evolution and the formation of the universe itself.

Stellar Evolution: The Life Stages of Stars

Like all living beings, stars go through a life cycle with distinct stages. From birth to death, they undergo fascinating transformations, each phase contributing to the cosmic drama unfolding in the universe. Let's take a closer look at the stages of stellar evolution.

1. Protostar: As we discussed earlier, this is the initial phase of a star's life, where it forms from a collapsing cloud of gas and dust. The protostar is not yet generating energy through fusion but is steadily growing in size and mass.

2. Main Sequence: The star enters the main sequence phase, where it fuses hydrogen into helium at its core, releasing energy and radiating light. This phase is characterized by a stable equilibrium between gravity and radiation pressure. The star will remain on the main sequence until it exhausts its core hydrogen fuel.

3. Red Giant/Supergiant: As a star exhausts its hydrogen fuel, its core contracts, causing the outer layers to expand and the star to swell in size. This phase is called the red giant phase for lower-mass stars and the red supergiant phase for more massive ones. During this phase, the star's outer layers cool and become enriched with heavier elements.

4. Planetary Nebula/Supernova: In the final stages of their lives, stars undergo dramatic transformations. For lower-mass stars, the outer layers are expelled, creating a beautiful shell of gas and dust known as a planetary nebula. The expelled material enriches the interstellar medium with heavy elements, which will be incorporated into future generations of stars and planetary systems. For more massive stars, the core collapse triggers a cataclysmic explosion called a supernova, releasing an immense amount of energy and dispersing heavy elements into space.

5. White Dwarf/Neutron Star/Black Hole: After the planetary nebula or supernova event, the remaining core of the star can take one of several paths. For lower-mass stars, the core collapses into a dense, hot white dwarf—a stellar remnant supported by electron degeneracy pressure. White dwarfs gradually cool over billions of years, eventually becoming black dwarfs.

In more massive stars, the core collapse leads to the formation of either a neutron star or, in the case of extreme mass, a black hole—a region of spacetime with gravity so strong that nothing can escape its pull. Neutron stars are incredibly dense remnants composed mainly of neutrons, while black holes are characterized by their gravitational singularity and event horizon.

Supernovae: Celestial Explosions

Among the most awe-inspiring events in the universe are supernovae—the explosive deaths of massive stars. When a star several times more massive than our Sun exhausts its nuclear fuel, its core collapses under its own gravity, triggering a cataclysmic explosion. For a brief moment, the supernova outshines an entire galaxy, releasing an astonishing amount of energy and synthesizing heavy elements, which are scattered into space.

Supernovae play a crucial role in the cosmic cycle of matter. These powerful explosions disperse the enriched materials—such as carbon, oxygen, and iron—into the surrounding interstellar medium, where they become part of future generations of stars and planetary systems. They are the cosmic alchemists, responsible for the creation of the building blocks of life.

Type II supernovae occur when massive stars, at least eight times the mass of the Sun, reach the end of their lives. The core collapse triggers a rebound, resulting in an explosive shockwave that tears the star apart. Type Ia supernovae, on the other hand, occur in binary star systems where a white dwarf accretes mass from a companion star, crossing a critical threshold and detonating in a thermonuclear explosion.

These cataclysmic events leave behind remnants that continue to influence the cosmos. Supernova remnants, such as the famous Crab Nebula, are expansive structures of gas and dust that carry the imprint of the stellar explosion. These remnants become stellar nurseries for the formation of new generations of stars, perpetuating the cosmic cycle of life and death.

Neutron Stars: Cosmic Densities

In the aftermath of a supernova, a remarkable cosmic entity can be born—a neutron star. Neutron stars are the incredibly dense remnants of massive stars, packing the mass of a few Suns into a sphere with a diameter of only a few kilometers. These objects are so dense that a teaspoon of neutron star material would weigh billions of tons.

Neutron stars possess mind-boggling properties. Their intense gravitational fields create a phenomenon called time dilation, where time appears to slow down for an outside observer. They also exhibit rapid rotation, emitting beams of radiation that we observe as pulsars—a type of cosmic lighthouse. Neutron stars are natural laboratories for studying extreme physics and provide valuable insights into the fundamental nature of matter and gravity.

Black Holes: Cosmic Abysses

Among the most mysterious and enigmatic objects in the universe are black holes—the cosmic abysses from which nothing, not even light, can escape. They form when the core of a massive star collapses under its own gravity, compressing matter into an infinitely dense singularity—a point of infinite density and zero volume.

Black holes exert a gravitational pull so strong that they warp spacetime, creating a region of no return called the event horizon. Beyond this point, the gravitational force is so intense that not even light can escape, making black holes invisible to direct observation. We can only infer their presence through their effects on surrounding matter and radiation.

Supermassive black holes, millions or even billions of times more massive than our Sun, reside at the centers of galaxies. They play a vital role in shaping galactic evolution, influencing the dynamics of stars, gas, and even the growth of galaxies themselves. The study of black holes continues to push the boundaries of our understanding of gravity and the fabric of spacetime.

Conclusion

Congratulations, young explorers! You have now witnessed the captivating life stages of stars, from their humble beginnings in stellar nurseries to their spectacular deaths as supernovae, neutron stars, or black holes. The universe's cosmic drama unfolds through the lives of these celestial performers, shaping the cosmic landscape we observe today.

In the next chapter, we will embark on an exhilarating journey through our own galaxy, the Milky Way. We will explore its structure, spiral arms, and galactic wonders, unraveling the secrets of our cosmic neighborhood. So, tighten your seatbelts and prepare for a thrilling ride through the vast expanse of our galactic home in *"Chapter 5: The Milky Way: Our Galactic Playground."*

Remember, the universe is brimming with wonders, waiting to be explored. Keep looking up, stay curious, and never stop reaching for the stars!

CHAPTER FIVE

The Milky Way: Our Galactic Playground

Introduction

Welcome, young explorers, to the heart of our cosmic neighborhood—the magnificent Milky Way galaxy. In the previous chapters, we marveled at the splendor of the night sky, delved into the mysteries of stars and their life cycles, and embarked on a journey through stellar nurseries and supernova explosions. Now, it's time to embark on an even deeper exploration of our galactic home. Get ready to traverse the vast expanse of the Milky Way, uncovering its intricate structure, celestial wonders, and hidden secrets. So, fasten your cosmic seatbelts and prepare for an extended adventure through the cosmic labyrinth in *"Chapter 5: The Milky Way: Our Galactic Playground."*

The Structure of the Milky Way

Imagine looking at the Milky Way from a distance—a breathtaking band of light stretching across the night sky. But what lies within that luminous tapestry? Our Milky Way is a majestic barred spiral galaxy, containing billions of stars, along with gas, dust, and elusive dark matter. Let's unravel the structure of our galactic home, revealing its remarkable components.

1. Galactic Disk: The primary visible component of the Milky Way is the galactic disk—an expansive, flattened structure resembling a cosmic pancake. The disk is home to most of the galaxy's stars, including our very own Sun, as well as interstellar gas and dust. It consists of various components, including the thin disk, where young stars and vibrant star-forming regions reside, and the thick disk, which hosts older stars.

2. *Galactic Bulge*: Nestled at the center of our galaxy lies the galactic bulge—a dense, elongated region where stars are densely packed together. This bulge takes on the shape of a bar, giving the Milky Way its classification as a barred spiral galaxy. Deep within the galactic bulge, a supermassive black hole known as Sagittarius A* resides, boasting a mass millions of times greater than that of our Sun.

3. *Spiral Arms*: Radiating outward from the galactic bulge are the awe-inspiring spiral arms of the Milky Way. These majestic arms are vast regions where stars, gas, and dust are arranged in sweeping spiral patterns. The Milky Way features four major spiral arms: the Perseus Arm, the Sagittarius Arm (which we are part of), the Norma Arm, and the Cygnus Arm. These arms are dynamic, perpetually in motion, and teeming with stellar clusters, nebulae, and star-forming regions.

Stellar Nurseries and Star Formation

Within the spiral arms of the Milky Way, hidden among the interstellar dust and gas, lie the birthplaces of new stars—stellar nurseries that foster the creation of celestial beacons. Let's delve into the process of star formation and explore these cosmic cradles of creation.

1. *Molecular Clouds:* Star formation begins within colossal molecular clouds—dense concentrations of gas and dust spread throughout the galaxy. These clouds primarily consist of molecular hydrogen (H_2), with traces of other molecules like carbon monoxide (CO) and water (H_2O). The gravitational collapse of a small region within a molecular cloud initiates the process of star birth.

2. *Protostars*: As a region within a molecular cloud collapses under its gravitational pull, it forms a protostar—a dense, hot core surrounded by a rotating disk of gas and dust. The protostar steadily accumulates mass from the surrounding material, growing in size and temperature. Intense heat and pressure at the protostar's core ignite nuclear fusion, marking the birth of a star.

3. *Main Sequence Stars:* When the protostar's core reaches a temperature of around 10 million degrees Celsius, nuclear fusion reactions of hydrogen atoms into helium atoms commence. At this point, the protostar enters the main sequence phase, where it will spend the majority of its life, steadily emitting energy through the fusion of hydrogen in its core. The exact path a star takes on the main sequence depends on its initial mass.

4. Stellar Evolution: Stars evolve and transform throughout their lifetimes, with their fate determined by their mass. Massive stars burn through their fuel quickly, leading to shorter lifespans and spectacular explosive events like supernovae. On the other hand, lower-mass stars, like our Sun, have longer lifetimes, gradually exhausting their hydrogen fuel before transitioning into red giants and eventually shedding their outer layers as planetary nebulae.

Mapping the Milky Way

Charting the intricacies of the Milky Way presents a formidable challenge for astronomers. How do we unravel the mysteries of its structure, composition, and dynamics? Over the years, scientists have employed various methods and technologies to map our galactic home and deepen our understanding of its awe-inspiring nature.

1. Star Counts: One of the earliest methods of mapping the Milky Way relied on star counts. By observing the density and distribution of stars in different directions, astronomers could infer the shape and structure of our galaxy. However, this method had limitations due to the obscuration caused by interstellar dust and the inability to observe stars in regions blocked by the galactic plane.

2. Radio Astronomy: The advent of radio telescopes revolutionized our understanding of the Milky Way. By detecting radio waves emitted by neutral atomic hydrogen (H I), astronomers were able to map the distribution of gas throughout the galaxy. This provided valuable insights into the spiral structure, density waves, and the connection between star formation and the interstellar medium.

3. Infrared Surveys: Infrared observations have proven indispensable in mapping the Milky Way, allowing us to penetrate the veil of interstellar dust and observe objects hidden from visible light. Surveys such as the Two Micron All-Sky Survey (2MASS) and the Wide-field Infrared Survey

Explorer (WISE) have provided detailed maps of the galaxy, highlighting the locations of stellar nurseries, dust lanes, and star clusters.

4. Gaia Mission: In recent years, the European Space Agency's Gaia mission has transformed our understanding of the Milky Way. Gaia is an astrometry satellite that precisely measures the positions, distances, and motions of over a billion stars in our galaxy. This extraordinary catalog of stellar data has enabled astronomers to create a three-dimensional map of the Milky Way, revealing its structure, dynamics, and the distribution of stars in unprecedented detail.

The Milky Way's Galactic Wonders

The Milky Way serves as a celestial playground, where countless wonders await discovery. Within its vast expanse, we encounter a myriad of cosmic marvels—each one offering a glimpse into the captivating nature of our galactic home. Let's embark on a grand cosmic tour and explore some of the remarkable features found within the Milky Way.

1. Open Clusters: Open clusters are stellar communities, consisting of a group of stars that formed from the same molecular cloud. These clusters vary in size, containing anywhere from a few dozen to a few thousand stars. Examples of open clusters include the Pleiades and the Beehive Cluster. These clusters are relatively young and often harbor hot, massive stars, making them excellent laboratories for studying stellar evolution.

2. Globular Clusters: Unlike open clusters, globular clusters are ancient and densely packed conglomerates of stars. These clusters contain hundreds of thousands, or even millions, of stars bound together by gravity. They form a spherical halo around the galactic center and are located outside the galactic disk. Notable examples of globular clusters include Omega Centauri and the Hercules Cluster (M13). Studying these clusters provides valuable insights into the early stages of galaxy formation and the evolution of stars.

3. Nebulae: Nebulae are vast clouds of gas and dust scattered throughout the Milky Way. They come in various forms, including emission nebulae, reflection nebulae, and dark nebulae. Emission nebulae, such as the Orion Nebula, are illuminated by nearby stars, while reflection nebulae, like the famous Witch Head Nebula, reflect the light of nearby stars. Dark nebulae, such as the Coalsack Nebula, appear as regions of dense obscuring dust.

Nebulae serve as stellar nurseries, fostering the birth of new stars, and offer magnificent opportunities to study the processes of star formation.

4. Supernova Remnants: Scattered throughout the Milky Way are the remnants of supernova explosions—a testament to the dramatic deaths of massive stars. These remnants, such as the Crab Nebula and the Veil Nebula, are vast and expanding shells of gas and dust. They offer a window into the cataclysmic events that shape our galaxy, dispersing heavy elements into the interstellar medium and enriching it with the building blocks of future stars and planets.

5. Black Holes and Neutron Stars: Hidden within the depths of the galactic bulge and dispersed throughout the spiral arms of the Milky Way, lie the remnants of massive stars—black holes and neutron stars. These enigmatic objects, born from the fiery deaths of their progenitors, continue to captivate astronomers. Black holes, with their intense gravitational pull, challenge our understanding of the fabric of spacetime, while neutron stars, with their ultra-dense cores, offer insights into the physics of extreme conditions. These stellar remnants are windows into the evolution of galaxies and the mysteries of the universe.

Conclusion

Congratulations, young explorers, for delving deep into the captivating wonders of the Milky Way—the spiral arms, the galactic bulge, and the stellar nurseries within. We've unraveled the structure of our galactic home, from the expansive galactic disk to the bustling galactic bulge and the awe-inspiring spiral arms. Along the way, we've witnessed the remarkable birth of stars within molecular clouds, their evolution on the main sequence, and their transformation into red giants and planetary nebulae.

But our cosmic journey doesn't end here. In the next chapter, we will transcend the boundaries of the Milky Way and venture into the vast extragalactic realm, exploring distant galaxies, quasars, and the mind-boggling concept of an expanding universe. So, young explorers, prepare to set your sights beyond the Milky Way in *"Chapter 6: Beyond the Milky Way: Exploring the Extragalactic Universe."*

Remember, the Milky Way is not only our galactic address but also a playground of cosmic wonders. Keep your eyes to the sky, embrace the curiosity within you, and let the mysteries of the universe unfold before your inquisitive minds!

Beyond the Milky Way: Exploring the Extragalactic Universe

Introduction

Welcome, young explorers, to the gateway of the cosmos. In the previous chapters, we delved into the vast expanse of our home galaxy, the Milky Way, unraveling its structure, stellar nurseries, and breathtaking wonders. But now, it's time to embark on an extraordinary journey beyond the familiar boundaries of our galactic playground. Brace yourselves as we traverse the unfathomable distances of the extragalactic universe, where mind-boggling discoveries and celestial wonders await in *"Chapter 6: Beyond the Milky Way: Exploring the Extragalactic Universe."*

The Great Debate: The Nature of Spiral Nebulae

Before we dive into the depths of the extragalactic realm, let's rewind time to a fascinating chapter in the history of astronomy—the Great Debate. In the early 20th century, astronomers were embroiled in a heated debate over the nature of spiral nebulae—vast, swirling clouds resembling pinwheels seen throughout the night sky.

1. Island Universes: On one side of the debate stood the proponents of the "island universe" hypothesis. They argued that spiral nebulae were distant galaxies similar to our own Milky Way, composed of billions of stars. This notion suggested that the universe extended far beyond the confines of our galaxy, filled with countless other galaxies.

2. *Nebulae within the Milky Way*: On the opposing side were astronomers who believed that spiral nebulae were mere extensions of our own Milky Way—a collection of gas and dust within our galactic neighborhood. According to this viewpoint, the universe consisted solely of our galaxy and did not extend beyond its boundaries.

The resolution to this debate came in the form of groundbreaking observations and scientific advancements. Let's explore the key discoveries that cemented the island universe hypothesis and expanded our understanding of the extragalactic universe.

Edwin Hubble and the Expanding Universe

One name stands out among the pioneers who revolutionized our perception of the cosmos—Edwin Hubble. Using the 100-inch Hooker Telescope at Mount Wilson Observatory, Hubble made groundbreaking observations that reshaped our understanding of the universe.

1. *Cepheid Variables:* Hubble utilized a specific type of variable star known as Cepheid variables to measure the distances to various spiral nebulae. These stars pulsate in a regular pattern, and their brightness fluctuations are directly related to their intrinsic luminosities. By comparing the observed brightness of Cepheid variables in distant spiral nebulae with their known luminosities, Hubble determined their distances.

2. *Andromeda Nebula:* Hubble's observations of the Andromeda Nebula (now known as the Andromeda Galaxy) provided the decisive evidence in favor of the island universe hypothesis. By measuring the distance to the Andromeda Nebula, Hubble showed that it was far beyond the boundaries of our Milky Way, making it the closest spiral galaxy to us.

3. *Redshift and the Expanding Universe*: Hubble's most revolutionary discovery came from analyzing the light emitted by galaxies. He observed a systematic redshift—a shift towards longer wavelengths—in the spectra of galaxies. This redshift indicated that galaxies were moving away from us. Hubble formulated a simple law, now known as Hubble's Law, which states that the recessional velocity of a galaxy is proportional to its distance from us. This discovery led to the profound realization that the universe was not static but expanding.

Types of Galaxies

Armed with the knowledge that spiral nebulae were, in fact, distant galaxies, astronomers embarked on a quest to classify and understand the diverse array of galaxies populating the extragalactic universe. Let's explore the major types of galaxies we've encountered so far:

1. Spiral Galaxies: Spirals are characterized by their prominent flattened disks, spiral arms, and a central bulge. These galaxies come in various subtypes, such as grand design spirals (with well-defined arms) and flocculent spirals (with more diffuse arms). Examples include the Andromeda Galaxy (M31) and our own Milky Way.

2. Elliptical Galaxies: Elliptical galaxies are shaped like ellipsoids, lacking the distinctive disk and spiral arms seen in spirals. They are typically composed of older stars and contain less gas and dust compared to spiral galaxies. Elliptical galaxies span a range of sizes, from small ellipticals to massive giants. Examples include M87 in the Virgo Cluster and M32 in the Local Group.

3. Irregular Galaxies: Irregular galaxies, as the name suggests, lack any distinct regular shape. They often exhibit chaotic and asymmetric structures, with ongoing star formation activity. These galaxies can be small or large and are sometimes the result of galactic interactions or mergers. The Large Magellanic Cloud (LMC) and the Small Magellanic Cloud (SMC) are examples of irregular galaxies.

4. Lenticular Galaxies: Lenticular galaxies, or S0 galaxies, have a disk-like structure similar to spirals but lack the prominent spiral arms. They are often described as intermediate between elliptical and spiral galaxies. Lenticular galaxies have less interstellar matter and lower star formation rates compared to spirals. An example is the Sombrero Galaxy (M104).

Galaxy Clusters and Superclusters

As we venture further into the extragalactic universe, we encounter vast structures that defy comprehension—galaxy clusters and superclusters. These gargantuan cosmic webs are composed of hundreds to thousands of galaxies, bound together by gravity. Let's delve into their intriguing properties:

1. Galaxy Clusters: Galaxy clusters are the largest gravitationally bound structures in the universe. They consist of numerous galaxies, hot gas, and dark matter. The galaxies within a cluster interact gravitationally and move through the cluster at high speeds. Some galaxy clusters exhibit impressive phenomena like galaxy collisions, gas heating, and the formation of powerful radio sources. Examples of galaxy clusters include the Coma Cluster, the Virgo Cluster, and the Fornax Cluster.

2. Superclusters: Superclusters are even larger structures that encompass multiple galaxy clusters. They represent the largest coherent structures in the universe, spanning hundreds of millions of light-years. Superclusters are interconnected by vast cosmic filaments, which are long, thread-like structures composed of dark matter and gas. The Laniakea Supercluster, which encompasses our Local Group and several nearby galaxy clusters, is one such awe-inspiring supercluster.

Active Galactic Nuclei and Quasars

As we explore the extragalactic universe, we encounter celestial powerhouses that push the boundaries of what we thought was possible—active galactic nuclei (AGNs) and quasars. These cosmic beacons emit prodigious amounts of energy, captivating astronomers with their extraordinary properties.

1. Active Galactic Nuclei (AGNs): AGNs are compact regions at the centers of galaxies that exhibit high luminosity across the electromagnetic spectrum. They arise from the accretion of mass onto a supermassive black hole residing in the galactic nucleus. AGNs display various phenomena, including powerful jets, intense X-ray emission, and rapidly varying brightness. Examples of AGNs include Seyfert galaxies, radio galaxies, and blazars.

2. Quasars: Quasars, short for "quasi-stellar radio sources," are the most energetic and distant members of the AGN family. These brilliant objects, often found at the centers of young galaxies, emit prodigious amounts of radiation. Quasars were first discovered as point sources, resembling stars, but their extraordinary spectra and extreme redshifts revealed their extragalactic nature. They offer a glimpse into the early stages of the universe's evolution, with some quasars dating back to when the universe was less than a billion years old.

Conclusion

Congratulations, young explorers, for venturing beyond the boundaries of our Milky Way and embracing the extragalactic wonders that await us. In this chapter, we unraveled the historic Great Debate, which solidified the concept of distant galaxies and expanded our cosmic horizons. We explored the breathtaking diversity of galaxies, from the elegant spirals to the enigmatic irregulars, and uncovered the vast structures of galaxy clusters and superclusters.

We also encountered the awe-inspiring powerhouses of the extragalactic universe—active galactic nuclei and quasars—where supermassive black holes reign supreme. These cosmic phenomena challenge our understanding of the universe and offer glimpses into its early stages.

But our journey through the extragalactic realm is far from over. In the next chapter, we will embark on a voyage to unravel the mysteries of dark matter and dark energy, two enigmatic components that dominate the universe's composition and expansion. Get ready, young explorers, for *"Chapter 7: Unveiling the Dark Universe: Dark Matter and Dark Energy."*

Remember, the extragalactic universe beckons us with its celestial marvels and mysteries. Keep your curiosity aflame, and let the wonders of the cosmos guide your quest for knowledge!

CHAPTER SEVEN

Unveiling the Dark Universe: Dark Matter and Dark Energy

Introduction

Welcome, young explorers, to the enigmatic depths of the universe. In our previous chapters, we marveled at the wonders of galaxies, explored the vast structures of galaxy clusters, and encountered the powerhouses of active galactic nuclei and quasars. But as we journey further, we confront the mysteries that shroud the cosmos—dark matter and dark energy. Brace yourselves for an extraordinary voyage into *"Chapter 7: Unveiling the Dark Universe: Dark Matter and Dark Energy."*

The Cosmic Puzzle: Dark Matter

1. Galactic Rotation Curves: Our quest to understand the nature of dark matter begins within our own galactic neighborhood. Astronomers have long observed that the rotation curves of galaxies defy the predictions of classical physics. According to the laws of gravity, the outer regions of a galaxy should orbit more slowly than the inner regions. However, observations revealed that stars and gas in galaxies were moving at relatively constant speeds, suggesting the presence of unseen matter—a phenomenon attributed to dark matter.

The dark matter's gravitational pull counteracts the gravitational force from visible matter, keeping stars and gas in the outer regions of galaxies in stable orbits. The nature of dark matter remains elusive, as it does not interact with electromagnetic radiation and remains invisible to our telescopes.

2. *Gravitational Lensing:* Another line of evidence supporting the existence of dark matter comes from gravitational lensing. When light from distant galaxies passes through the gravitational field of a massive object, such as a galaxy cluster, it gets bent and distorted, creating multiple images or arcs. The observed gravitational lensing effect is far greater than what can be accounted for by the visible matter alone, providing strong evidence for the existence of dark matter.

Gravitational lensing not only confirms the presence of dark matter but also allows astronomers to map its distribution within galaxy clusters. By studying the distortions in the background light, scientists can infer the mass and spatial distribution of dark matter, revealing its significant role in shaping the large-scale structure of the universe.

3. *Cosmic Microwave Background:* The cosmic microwave background (CMB) radiation—the remnant glow from the early universe—also provides insights into the existence of dark matter. Tiny fluctuations in the CMB radiation, imprinted shortly after the Big Bang, serve as a cosmic time capsule. These fluctuations provide a snapshot of the universe's early density variations.

Through precise measurements of the CMB, scientists have determined the overall composition of the universe. They found that ordinary matter, the stuff we're made of, accounts for only about 5% of the universe's energy density. The remaining 95% is made up of dark matter and dark energy. The CMB data confirms that dark matter plays a crucial role in the dynamics and structure formation of the universe.

The Enigmatic Dark Energy

1. *Cosmic Expansion:* The story of dark energy begins with the unexpected revelation that the expansion of the universe is not slowing down due to gravity but, in fact, accelerating. Observations of distant supernovae in the late 1990s revealed that these cosmic explosions were fainter than expected, indicating that the universe's expansion was accelerating under the influence of an unknown force—dark energy.

This discovery turned the conventional understanding of the universe on its head. Scientists were puzzled by the source of this repulsive force that counteracts gravity on cosmic scales.

2. Einstein's Cosmological Constant: The concept of dark energy can be traced back to Albert Einstein's general theory of relativity. Einstein introduced a cosmological constant, a term in his equations representing a repulsive force that counteracts gravity and keeps the universe static. However, when the expanding universe was discovered, Einstein discarded the cosmological constant as a blunder. Decades later, the discovery of cosmic acceleration brought it back into the spotlight.

The cosmological constant is now interpreted as a form of dark energy—a pervasive energy field that permeates space and drives the accelerated expansion of the universe. But the exact nature of dark energy remains one of the greatest mysteries in modern astrophysics.

3. Cosmic Microwave Background: Just as the CMB helped us understand dark matter, it also provides crucial insights into dark energy. The precise measurements of the CMB's temperature fluctuations reveal the expansion history of the universe and the density of its constituents. The observed patterns in the CMB support the existence of dark energy and its dominant role in the universe's dynamics.

The combination of observations, including the CMB data and measurements of supernovae, galaxy clusters, and the large-scale structure of the universe, paints a compelling picture of a universe dominated by dark matter and dark energy. While dark matter acts as the scaffolding, gravitationally attracting ordinary matter and providing the framework for structure formation, dark energy plays a transformative role, driving the accelerated expansion and shaping the cosmic destiny.

Cosmic Interplay: Dark Matter and Dark Energy

The cosmic dance between dark matter and dark energy shapes the evolution of the universe on grand scales. While dark matter acts as the scaffolding, gravitationally attracting ordinary matter and providing the framework for structure formation, dark energy plays a transformative role, driving the accelerated expansion and shaping the cosmic destiny.

1. *Large-Scale Structure Formation:* Dark matter's gravitational pull dictates the formation of cosmic structures, from the vast cosmic web of galaxy filaments to the clustering of galaxies within galaxy clusters. Through computer simulations and observations, astronomers have unraveled the intricate interplay between dark matter and visible matter, revealing the cosmic tapestry that connects galaxies across billions of light-years.

By studying the distribution of galaxies and their motions within galaxy clusters, scientists can map the distribution of dark matter. These observations, combined with simulations, allow us to understand how dark matter influences the growth of cosmic structures over billions of years.

2. *The Fate of the Universe:* The combined influence of dark matter and dark energy holds the key to the universe's fate. Will the expansion continue unabated, leading to the "Big Freeze" scenario where galaxies drift apart, becoming isolated islands in an ever-expanding cosmic sea? Or will dark energy evolve, leading to a "Big Rip" scenario, tearing apart galaxies, stars, and even atoms in an exponential expansion?

The ultimate fate of the universe hinges on understanding the nature of dark energy and how it may evolve over cosmic time. Scientists are tirelessly exploring this mysterious force to decipher its properties and unravel the cosmic destiny that awaits us.

Conclusion

Congratulations, young explorers, for delving into the depths of the dark universe. In this chapter, we embarked on a quest to unravel the mysteries of dark matter and dark energy. We explored the evidence for dark matter's existence, from galactic rotation curves to gravitational lensing and the cosmic microwave background. We also uncovered the enigmatic nature of dark energy, from its role in cosmic expansion to its cosmic dance with dark matter.

But our exploration of the dark universe is far from over. In the next chapter, we will dive into the cosmic crucibles of star birth—the stellar nurseries that give rise to the spectacular variety of stars and their life cycles. Get ready, young explorers, for *"Chapter 8: Stellar Evolution: The Cosmic Life Cycle of Stars."*

Remember, the mysteries of the universe are vast, but with each discovery, we come closer to unraveling its secrets. Let your curiosity guide your journey as we continue our exploration of the cosmos!

Stellar Evolution: The Cosmic Life Cycle of Stars

Introduction

Welcome back, intrepid explorers, to the captivating realm of stars! In our previous chapters, we marveled at the grand structures of galaxies, uncovered the mysteries of dark matter and dark energy, and witnessed the birth of stars within giant molecular clouds. Now, it's time to embark on an even deeper journey into the cosmic life cycle of stars. Get ready to be astounded as we unravel the intricate processes that shape these celestial powerhouses in *"Chapter 8: Stellar Evolution: The Cosmic Life Cycle of Stars."*

Birth of Stars: Stellar Nurseries

1. Giant Molecular Clouds: Our journey commences within colossal interstellar clouds known as giant molecular clouds. These immense structures, spanning tens to hundreds of light-years, are composed of gas and dust—primordial ingredients crucial for star formation. Within these cosmic nurseries, gravity acts as the master sculptor, drawing together particles of gas and dust and triggering the birth of new stars.

Giant molecular clouds contain vast reservoirs of molecular hydrogen—the primary fuel for star formation. As regions within the cloud become denser due to gravity, they fragment into smaller clumps called molecular cores. These cores are the cradles where future stars will take shape.

2. Protostars: Within these molecular cores, the process of star formation commences. As the core contracts under gravity's pull, it heats up, eventually reaching temperatures where nuclear fusion can occur. At this stage, the young, forming star is known as a protostar. Surrounding the protostar is a rotating disk of material called a protoplanetary disk, from which planets may later form.

The protostar continues to grow by accreting matter from its surrounding disk. As material falls onto the protostar, it releases gravitational potential energy in the form of heat and light. However, the protostar's intense radiation and outflowing stellar winds make direct observation challenging. Nonetheless, using infrared telescopes and other instruments, astronomers can peer through the dusty veil and witness the early stages of stellar evolution.

3. Pre-Main Sequence Stars: As the protostar continues to accumulate mass from its surrounding disk, it evolves into what is known as a pre-main sequence star. During this phase, the star is not yet in equilibrium—it undergoes significant changes in size, temperature, and luminosity over relatively short timescales.

Pre-main sequence stars generate energy through gravitational contraction—the release of stored potential energy as the star shrinks. As the star contracts, its central temperature rises, eventually reaching a point where the core becomes hot enough for nuclear fusion to ignite. This marks the beginning of the star's journey onto the main sequence.

Main Sequence Stars: The Stellar Powerhouses

1. Hydrostatic Equilibrium: Once a star reaches the main sequence, it achieves a delicate balance between the inward pull of gravity and the outward pressure generated by nuclear fusion. This equilibrium, known as hydrostatic equilibrium, is crucial for a star to maintain a stable size and luminosity.

Main sequence stars come in a range of sizes and temperatures. The mass of a star determines its size and temperature on the main sequence—the more massive the star, the larger and hotter it is. For instance, blue supergiant stars like Rigel are several times more massive than the Sun, while red dwarf stars are smaller and cooler.

2. *Nuclear Fusion*: At the core of a main sequence star, a remarkable process called nuclear fusion powers the star. Through the fusion of hydrogen atoms, stars unleash tremendous amounts of energy. The core of a main sequence star serves as a natural nuclear reactor, where hydrogen atoms combine to form helium, releasing energy in the process.

In stars like our Sun, hydrogen fusion occurs through the proton-proton chain reaction. Deeper within more massive stars, a different fusion process called the CNO cycle dominates. These nuclear fusion reactions release energy in the form of light and heat, providing the necessary pressure to resist the inward pull of gravity and maintain hydrostatic equilibrium.

3. *Stellar Stability*: While main sequence stars appear relatively stable, they are not completely static. Small fluctuations in a star's core temperature or density can lead to adjustments in the fusion rate, compensating for the changes and restoring equilibrium. This process helps to maintain a star's stable size, luminosity, and overall appearance on the main sequence.

However, main sequence stars are not eternal. As hydrogen in the core becomes depleted, stars undergo gradual changes that will ultimately shape their future evolution. The duration of a star's stay on the main sequence depends on its mass—the more massive the star, the shorter its main sequence lifetime.

The Stellar Endgame: Stellar Death and Beyond

1. *Red Giants and Supergiants*: As hydrogen fusion in the core dwindles, a star's internal structure begins to change. In the case of stars like our Sun, the core contracts while the outer envelope expands, transforming the star into a red giant. Red giants are much larger and cooler than their main sequence counterparts, appearing red in color.

In more massive stars, the core contraction triggers a helium fusion process, causing the star to evolve into a red supergiant—a truly gargantuan celestial object. Red supergiants, like Betelgeuse in the constellation Orion, are among the largest stars known, stretching far beyond the orbits of planets in our solar system.

2. *Planetary Nebulae*: After the red giant or supergiant phase, lower-mass stars undergo a fascinating transformation. The outer layers of the star are expelled into space, creating a vibrant, glowing cloud of gas and dust known as a planetary nebula. Despite its name, a planetary nebula has nothing to do with planets; the term originated from early observations that gave these nebulae a planet-like appearance.

At the heart of a planetary nebula lies a remnant known as a white dwarf—a dense, hot stellar core composed primarily of carbon and oxygen. White dwarfs are the final evolutionary stage for stars with masses similar to or lower than that of our Sun. These stellar remnants slowly cool over billions of years, fading away as they relinquish their stored thermal energy.

3. *Supernovae*: The fate of massive stars is far more dramatic. As red supergiants exhaust their nuclear fuel, their cores collapse under the crushing weight of gravity. This collapse initiates an extraordinary cataclysmic event—a supernova explosion. Supernovae release an incredible amount of energy, briefly outshining an entire galaxy.

Supernovae play a pivotal role in the universe, as they forge heavy elements through nucleosynthesis and disperse them into space. These elements, including the building blocks of life, become the raw materials for future generations of stars and planetary systems. Supernovae also produce shockwaves that can trigger the formation of new stars and influence the dynamics of galaxies.

4. *Neutron Stars and Black Holes:* In the aftermath of a supernova, the core of a massive star collapses further. If the core mass is between about 1.4 and 3 times the mass of the Sun, it becomes incredibly dense, giving birth to a neutron star. Neutron stars are remnants packed with more mass than the Sun but compressed into a sphere only about 20 kilometers (12 miles) in diameter.

For stars with even higher masses, the core collapse is so intense that not even neutrons can resist the pull of gravity. These stellar remnants collapse to form black holes—objects with such strong gravitational fields that nothing, not even light, can escape their grasp. Black holes continue to intrigue astronomers, posing fascinating questions about the nature of spacetime and the fundamental laws of physics.

Conclusion

Congratulations, young cosmic explorers, for delving deep into the wondrous journey of stellar evolution! In this chapter, we witnessed the awe-inspiring birth of stars within giant molecular clouds, marveled at the radiant power of main sequence stars, beheld the majestic transformations into red giants and supergiants, witnessed the creation of planetary nebulae and white dwarfs, and stood in awe of the explosive grandeur of supernovae and the enigmatic formations of neutron stars and black holes.

But fear not, for our voyage through the stellar cosmos is far from over. In the next chapter, we shall set our sights beyond our solar system to explore the captivating realm of exoplanets—worlds orbiting distant stars. Brace yourselves, young explorers, for *"Chapter 9: Exoplanets: Unveiling the Secrets of Alien Worlds."*

Remember, the universe is a tapestry of cosmic wonders, and each star has its own unique story to tell. Keep your eyes on the night sky, and let the grand symphony of stars ignite your imagination as we continue our cosmic odyssey!

CHAPTER NINE

Exoplanets: Unveiling the Secrets of Alien Worlds

Introduction

Welcome, intrepid explorers, to the captivating realm of exoplanets—realms beyond our solar system that hold the tantalizing promise of otherworldly discoveries. In our previous chapters, we marveled at the grandeur of stars and witnessed the captivating dance of stellar evolution. Now, we embark on an extraordinary expedition to unravel the mysteries of exoplanets and delve into *"Chapter 9: Exoplanets: Unveiling the Secrets of Alien Worlds."*

The Quest for Exoplanets: A Historical Perspective

1. The Pioneers: Before we plunge into the captivating world of exoplanets, let's pay homage to the trailblazers who laid the foundation for this incredible scientific frontier. In the 1990s, the first exoplanets were discovered by astronomers using the radial velocity method, which detects the tiny wobbles induced in a star by the gravitational pull of an orbiting planet. This groundbreaking discovery revolutionized our understanding of planetary systems and ignited a quest to uncover the vast diversity of exoplanetary worlds.

2. Transit Method: Another remarkable technique used to detect exoplanets is the transit method. This method relies on observing a slight dimming of a star's light when a planet passes in front of it, causing a temporary eclipse-like event. This subtle change in brightness can provide valuable insights into the size, orbit, and atmosphere of the transiting exoplanet. The transit method has proven particularly fruitful in identifying exoplanets orbiting close to their host stars.

3. *Direct Imaging*: Capturing the faint light of an exoplanet directly is a monumental challenge due to the overwhelming glare of the parent star. However, advancements in technology and innovative observing techniques have allowed astronomers to push the boundaries of direct imaging. By using specialized instruments that block out the star's light or using advanced adaptive optics systems, astronomers have managed to directly capture images of a few select exoplanets, providing valuable visual data.

4. *Microlensing and Gravitational Lensing*: Microlensing is a remarkable phenomenon that occurs when the gravity of a foreground star bends and magnifies the light of a distant background star. This bending effect can also occur due to an intervening exoplanet, resulting in a temporary brightening of the background star. By studying these microlensing events, astronomers can infer the presence of exoplanets, even if they cannot directly observe them.

Characterizing Exoplanets: Unraveling Their Secrets

1. *Exoplanet Atmospheres:* The composition and properties of an exoplanet's atmosphere hold crucial clues about its formation, evolution, and potential habitability. Spectroscopic observations allow astronomers to study the chemical composition of exoplanet atmospheres by analyzing the light that passes through them. By detecting specific signatures in the spectrum, such as the presence of water vapor, carbon dioxide, or methane, scientists can infer the atmospheric conditions and potential habitability of these distant worlds.

2. *Habitability and the Goldilocks Zone:* The search for habitable exoplanets centers around the concept of the Goldilocks Zone, also known as the habitable zone. This is the region around a star where conditions are just right—neither too hot nor too cold—for the existence of liquid water, a crucial ingredient for life as we know it. By identifying exoplanets within this zone, astronomers can prioritize their investigations and focus on worlds that may harbor the potential for life.

3. *Exoplanet Diversity*: The diversity of exoplanets has astounded astronomers, challenging conventional notions of planetary formation and migration. From gas giants close to their host stars to rocky worlds in tight orbits, and from scorching hot planets to icy, distant giants, the exoplanet catalog continues to grow, unveiling a multitude of intriguing and sometimes bizarre worlds. By studying their characteristics, such as mass, size, and density, astronomers aim to classify and understand the vast range of exoplanet types.

4. *Exomoons*: Just as moons play a vital role in our solar system, exomoons—moons orbiting exoplanets—offer unique opportunities for supporting life and maintaining habitable conditions. The detection and characterization of exomoons present significant challenges due to their small size and the complexity of their interactions within exoplanetary systems. Nonetheless, ongoing research and future missions hold the promise of unveiling these enigmatic worlds.

Beyond Detection: Characterizing Habitable Worlds

1. *The Search for Biosignatures*: The ultimate quest in the study of exoplanets is the search for biosignatures—indications of life or its byproducts within an exoplanet's atmosphere. Detecting biomarkers such as oxygen, ozone, methane, and other chemical imbalances could provide strong evidence for the existence of life beyond Earth. Upcoming telescopes, such as the James Webb Space Telescope, will revolutionize our ability to detect and study these tantalizing signatures.

2. *Technological Advances*: The hunt for exoplanets and their potential habitability has spurred remarkable advancements in technology and instrumentation. From space-based telescopes equipped with cutting-edge detectors to ground-based observatories employing adaptive optics, interferometry, and coronagraphs, astronomers are continuously pushing the boundaries of what is possible. These technological breakthroughs open up new realms of exploration and pave the way for future discoveries.

3. *Future Missions*: Exciting missions on the horizon promise to revolutionize our understanding of exoplanets. The James Webb Space Telescope, scheduled for launch in the near future, will provide unprecedented capabilities for characterizing exoplanet atmospheres.

Additionally, the upcoming PLATO mission, the Nancy Grace Roman Space Telescope, and the ARIEL mission will further expand our exoplanet census and enable detailed investigations of exoplanet systems.

Conclusion

Bravo, intrepid cosmic adventurers, for venturing into the captivating realm of exoplanets! In this chapter, we delved into the historical milestones of exoplanet discovery, explored the diverse methods used to detect and study these alien worlds, and unraveled the secrets of their atmospheres, habitability, and diversity. The ongoing quest to uncover the mysteries of exoplanets has transformed our understanding of the cosmos and opened up a new era of exploration.

But our cosmic journey is far from over. In the next chapter, we shall voyage through the majestic realm of galaxies, unveiling their breathtaking beauty and unraveling the cosmic tapestry that binds them together. Prepare yourselves, young explorers, for *"Chapter 10: Galaxies: Islands of Stars in the Cosmic Ocean."*

Remember, the universe brims with countless wonders, and exoplanets are just a glimpse into the vast tapestry of cosmic possibilities. Keep your eyes on the stars, for they hold the keys to unlocking the secrets of our place in the cosmos.

CHAPTER TEN

Galaxies: Islands of Stars in the Cosmic Ocean

Introduction

Welcome, intrepid cosmic explorers, to the magnificent realm of galaxies! In our previous chapters, we delved into the mysteries of stars, planets, and exoplanets, uncovering the wonders of the universe. Now, we embark on an epic journey to unravel the secrets of galaxies in *"Chapter 10: Galaxies: Islands of Stars in the Cosmic Ocean."*

The Vastness of Galaxies

1. Defining Galaxies: Before we embark on our exploration, let's understand what exactly a galaxy is. A galaxy is a vast ensemble of stars, gas, dust, and dark matter, bound together by gravity. These cosmic islands come in various shapes and sizes, ranging from majestic spirals with their graceful arms to elliptical galaxies with their smooth, football-like shapes, and irregular galaxies with their chaotic and peculiar forms. Our own Milky Way is a beautiful spiral galaxy, home to billions of stars.

2. The Discovery of Galaxies: The true nature of galaxies as distinct entities beyond our own was revealed through the pioneering work of astronomers like Edwin Hubble. In the early 20th century, Hubble's observations using powerful telescopes unveiled a universe teeming with countless galaxies, each a universe in its own right. This monumental discovery forever transformed our understanding of the cosmos and paved the way for the study of these remarkable structures.

3. Galactic Neighborhoods: Galaxies rarely exist in isolation. They tend to cluster together, forming cosmic neighborhoods that are bound by gravity. These galactic congregations provide rich environments for interactions and dynamic processes. Our galactic neighborhood, known as the Local Group, consists of around 54 galaxies, including the Milky Way and our closest cosmic companion, the Andromeda Galaxy. Exploring these galactic neighborhoods offers insights into the intricate web of cosmic interactions.

Unveiling the Diversity of Galaxies

1. Spiral Galaxies: Let us begin our exploration by diving into the mesmerizing world of spiral galaxies. These galaxies boast exquisite, swirling arms that emanate from a central bulge. Within their grand design, new stars are born, and cosmic spectacles unfold, such as supernovae and vibrant star-forming regions. The study of spiral galaxies provides valuable insights into the mechanisms of star formation, galactic structure, and the interplay of stellar populations.

2. Elliptical Galaxies: In stark contrast to the graceful spirals, elliptical galaxies present a different face of the galactic realm. These galaxies appear smooth and featureless, lacking the distinct spiral arms. Composed predominantly of aging stars, elliptical galaxies have exhausted their gas reservoirs for forming new stars. Their shapes, influenced by gravity, reflect the collective motion of their stars. Understanding the formation and evolution of elliptical galaxies offers a glimpse into the cosmic processes that shape these enigmatic structures.

3. Irregular Galaxies: As the name suggests, irregular galaxies defy traditional classifications. They exhibit irregular shapes, often marked by clumps, streams, and tidal tails. Irregular galaxies can arise from gravitational interactions and mergers between galaxies or from intense bursts of star formation. These cosmic rebels provide valuable insights into the dynamic nature of the universe, revealing the turbulent events that shape galactic evolution.

4. Dwarf Galaxies: Though small in size, dwarf galaxies play a significant role in the cosmic ecosystem. These diminutive companions often orbit larger galaxies like the Milky Way and Andromeda, contributing to the galactic tapestry. Dwarf galaxies serve as natural laboratories for studying the processes of galaxy formation, the distribution of dark matter, and the interplay between galaxies in their cosmic neighborhoods.

Exploring Galactic Evolution

1. Galactic Collisions: Galaxies are not static entities; they evolve and interact over cosmic timescales. Galactic collisions are cosmic encounters that reshape the structures of galaxies and ignite intense star formation. When galaxies collide, their gravitational interactions induce tidal forces, resulting in the distortion of their shapes, the formation of galactic tails, and the birth of new stars. These celestial dances hold the key to understanding the dynamism and evolutionary paths of galaxies.

2. Active Galactic Nuclei (AGNs): At the heart of many galaxies lies a supermassive black hole. When these black holes accrete matter from their surroundings, they unleash immense amounts of energy, giving rise to active galactic nuclei (AGNs). AGNs can outshine their host galaxies, emitting intense radiation across the electromagnetic spectrum. Studying AGNs enables us to probe the extreme physics near supermassive black holes and gain insights into the coevolution of galaxies and their central black holes.

3. Galactic Winds: Galaxies are not confined within their visible boundaries. They interact with their surroundings through powerful galactic winds—streams of particles propelled by energetic events like supernovae and starbursts. These galactic winds can carry gas, dust, and even heavy elements from the inner regions of galaxies into intergalactic space, shaping the larger cosmic ecosystem and enriching the galactic neighborhoods.

The Mysteries of Dark Matter and Dark Energy

1. Dark Matter: The presence of dark matter, an elusive and invisible substance, has a profound influence on galactic structure and evolution.

Dark matter outweighs ordinary matter by a significant margin, shaping the distribution of galaxies and providing the gravitational scaffolding that holds them together. Though its precise nature remains a mystery, scientists continue to search for clues to unlock the secrets of dark matter and its role in shaping the cosmic web.

2. Dark Energy: Dark energy is an even more enigmatic force that permeates the universe, driving its accelerated expansion. It counteracts the pull of gravity, pushing galaxies apart and stretching the very fabric of space. Unraveling the nature of dark energy is one of the most pressing challenges in modern cosmology and holds the key to understanding the ultimate fate of our universe.

Conclusion

Congratulations, bold cosmic explorers, for embarking on this grand adventure into the realm of galaxies! In this chapter, we marveled at the diverse shapes and structures of spiral, elliptical, and irregular galaxies. We uncovered the dynamic processes that shape galactic evolution, witnessed cosmic collisions, and delved into the mysteries of dark matter and dark energy.

But our cosmic odyssey is far from over. In the next chapter, brace yourselves for a thrilling encounter with the most enigmatic cosmic entities of all—black holes. *"Chapter 11: Black Holes: Portals to the Unknown"* will unveil the captivating secrets and mind-bending physics of these cosmic abysses.

Remember, young explorers, galaxies are the celestial beacons that illuminate the vast expanse of the universe. Each galaxy holds its own story, and by deciphering their secrets, we gain profound insights into the grand tapestry of cosmic evolution. Keep your eyes fixed on the stars as you voyage through the cosmos, and let the wonders of the universe ignite your curiosity and awe.

CHAPTER ELEVEN

Black Holes: Portals to the Unknown

Introduction

Welcome, fearless cosmic explorers, to the captivating realm of black holes! In our journey through the cosmos, we have marveled at the wonders of galaxies, stars, and planets. Now, we venture into the depths of space-time itself, where gravity reigns supreme. Prepare to be enthralled as we unlock the secrets of *"Chapter 11: Black Holes: Portals to the Unknown."*

Unveiling the Enigma of Black Holes

1. What is a Black Hole?: A black hole is a region in space where gravity is so incredibly strong that nothing, not even light, can escape its grasp. It is born from the remnants of massive stars that have exhausted their nuclear fuel and collapsed under their own gravitational pull. The boundary around a black hole, known as the event horizon, marks the point of no return.

2. Anatomy of a Black Hole: Black holes possess remarkable properties that defy our everyday understanding of physics. At their core lies the singularity, a point of infinite density and zero volume, where the laws of physics break down. Surrounding the singularity is the event horizon, which determines the size of the black hole and acts as an invisible barrier from which nothing can escape.

3. Types of Black Holes: Black holes come in different flavors, classified based on their mass and formation process. Stellar black holes form from the collapse of massive stars and can have a mass ranging from a few times that of our Sun to several tens of solar masses. Intermediate-mass black holes are a rarer type with masses between 100 and 100,000 times that of the Sun. Supermassive black holes, on the other hand, reside at the centers of galaxies and can have masses millions or even billions of times that of the Sun.

The Dance of Gravity: Understanding Black Hole Dynamics

1. Gravity's Grip: The force that shapes black holes is gravity, the curvature of space and time caused by mass and energy. As objects get closer to a black hole, the gravitational pull becomes increasingly stronger, leading to a phenomenon known as gravitational time dilation. Time near a black hole runs slower than in regions of weaker gravity, creating a fascinating interplay between space, time, and the behavior of matter.

2. Accretion Disks: As matter falls toward a black hole, it forms an accretion disk—a swirling disk of gas and dust that spirals around the event horizon. The intense gravitational forces generate friction and heat within the disk, causing it to emit copious amounts of energy, including X-rays and gamma rays. Accretion disks provide valuable insights into the dynamics of matter under extreme gravity and are often accompanied by spectacular cosmic phenomena, such as relativistic jets.

3. Relativistic Jets: Some black holes unleash powerful jets of energetic particles that shoot out into space at nearly the speed of light. These relativistic jets can extend for vast distances, stretching across thousands of light-years. The exact mechanism behind jet formation remains an active area of research, but it is believed to involve the interaction of intense magnetic fields with the black hole's accretion disk. Understanding relativistic jets allows us to probe the extreme physics near black holes and their impact on the surrounding cosmic environment.

4. Spacetime Warp: Black holes are not just objects that exert a strong gravitational pull; they also warp the fabric of space and time itself. The curvature of spacetime near a black hole causes light to follow curved paths, resulting in phenomena like gravitational lensing. Gravitational lensing allows astronomers to observe distant objects by bending the light around a black hole, effectively creating cosmic magnifying glasses.

The Cosmic Significance of Black Holes

1. Galactic Evolution: Supermassive black holes reside at the centers of galaxies, exerting a profound influence on their evolution. Through a process called feedback, black holes release enormous amounts of energy into their surroundings, regulating star formation and shaping the growth of galaxies. The interplay between black holes and galaxies is a crucial factor in understanding the cosmic dance of creation and destruction.

2. Gravitational Waves: Albert Einstein's theory of general relativity predicts that the movements of massive objects can create ripples in the fabric of space-time, known as gravitational waves. Black holes, with their tremendous masses and powerful gravitational fields, are prime sources of these waves. In recent years, the direct detection of gravitational waves has opened up a new window to observe and study black holes, providing unprecedented insights into their properties and cosmic interactions.

3. Black Hole Mysteries: Black holes still hold many mysteries that baffle scientists. For instance, the information paradox challenges our understanding of the preservation of information in the presence of a black hole's immense gravitational pull. The study of black holes also intersects with fundamental questions about the nature of space, time, and the ultimate limits of our current physical theories. Researchers continue to push the boundaries of knowledge in their quest to unravel the secrets of these cosmic enigmas.

Conclusion

Congratulations, intrepid cosmic adventurers, for delving into the mesmerizing world of black holes! In this chapter, we embarked on a thrilling journey to understand the nature and dynamics of these cosmic portals. We explored the anatomy of black holes, their powerful gravitational effects, and their cosmic significance, from galactic evolution to the detection of gravitational waves.

But our odyssey through the cosmos is not yet complete. Brace yourselves as we set our sights on *"Chapter 12: The Big Bang and the Birth of the Universe."* In this climactic chapter, we will unravel the mysteries of the universe's origins, the cosmic microwave background radiation, and the extraordinary expansion that set the stage for everything we see today.

Stay curious, young explorers, and let the allure of the unknown guide you as you traverse the cosmic landscape. The secrets of the universe await your unyielding curiosity and relentless quest for knowledge. Onward, towards the mysteries that lie beyond the event horizon!

CHAPTER TWELVE

The Big Bang and the Birth of the Universe

Introduction

Welcome, intrepid cosmic adventurers, to the grandest of cosmic tales—the story of the Big Bang and the birth of our universe! In our cosmic journey, we have explored the vastness of galaxies, witnessed the awe-inspiring dance of stars, delved into the mysteries of black holes, and unraveled the secrets of cosmic microwave background radiation. Now, we embark on an even deeper quest to understand the origins of it all. Prepare to be enthralled as we delve into the depths of *"Chapter 12: The Big Bang and the Birth of the Universe."*

The Prelude to Creation

1. Cosmic Puzzle Pieces: To comprehend the Big Bang, we must assemble the disparate pieces of evidence from various scientific disciplines. Concepts from astronomy, physics, cosmology, and particle physics converge to paint a comprehensive picture of our universe's remarkable journey. By examining the cosmic microwave background radiation, the distribution of galaxies, the expansion of the universe, and the behavior of fundamental particles, scientists have pieced together an intricate and awe-inspiring story of cosmic origins.

2. The Expanding Universe: One of the most foundational discoveries in modern cosmology is the observation that our universe is expanding.

Astronomer Edwin Hubble's groundbreaking observations in the 1920s revealed that galaxies are moving away from each other, suggesting that the universe is not static but in a state of constant flux. This realization laid the foundation for the Big Bang theory—a paradigm-shifting concept that forever changed our understanding of the cosmos and set the stage for our exploration of its origins.

The Birth of Space and Time

1. Inflation: In the earliest moments of the universe, a process known as inflation took place. This rapid and exponential expansion, driven by a peculiar form of energy, smoothed out irregularities and set the stage for the formation of structures we see today. Inflation not only explains the overall uniformity of our universe but also provides an elegant solution to the puzzles of cosmic microwave background radiation and large-scale structure.

2. Planck Epoch: As we journey back in time, we reach the Planck epoch—the earliest measurable moment in our universe's history. During this unfathomably brief period, the universe was governed by quantum physics, and the fundamental forces of nature were unified. Understanding the Planck epoch poses a profound challenge, as it requires reconciling the seemingly incompatible theories of quantum mechanics and general relativity.

The Fireball of Creation

1. The Hot, Dense Universe: Immediately following the Planck epoch, the universe was a seething cauldron of intense energy and unimaginable temperatures. As the universe expanded and cooled, it transitioned into an era dominated by particle interactions. Particles and antiparticles collided and annihilated each other, leaving behind a residue of photons and matter. This cosmic soup marked the transition from the era of quantum physics to the realm of classical physics.

2. *Nucleosynthesis*: Within the first few minutes after the Big Bang, the universe was hot enough to initiate a process called nucleosynthesis. Protons and neutrons collided, fusing together to form the building blocks of atomic nuclei. This era of nucleosynthesis was responsible for the production of the primordial elements—primarily hydrogen and helium—and left behind traces of lithium. It laid the foundation for the creation of all other elements in the universe through stellar fusion.

3. *Recombination*: As the universe continued to expand and cool, it entered a critical phase known as recombination. During this epoch, electrons combined with atomic nuclei to form neutral atoms, allowing photons to travel freely through space. The release of these photons, known as the cosmic microwave background radiation, provides a window into the early stages of the universe and offers valuable insights into its structure and composition.

The Cosmic Symphony Unveiled

1. *The Echo of Creation*: The cosmic microwave background radiation (CMB) is a testament to the primordial moments of our universe. Detected as faint radio waves permeating the cosmos, the CMB provides a snapshot of the universe when it was a mere 380,000 years old. By studying the fluctuations in temperature and density across the CMB, scientists gain profound insights into the seeds of cosmic structure, the expansion of the universe, and the conditions shortly after the Big Bang.

2. *The Birth of Galaxies*: Over billions of years, the primordial fluctuations imprinted in the cosmic microwave background radiation grew in density, giving rise to the formation of galaxies. Gravity played a pivotal role, causing matter to clump together and form structures of increasing complexity. Within these galaxies, stars ignited, forging the elements necessary for the emergence of life and providing the cosmic laboratories for the creation of heavier elements through stellar nucleosynthesis.

3. *Dark Matter and Dark Energy*: The cosmic symphony composed by the Big Bang is incomplete without acknowledging the enigmatic forces of dark matter and dark energy. Dark matter, which outweighs normal matter in the universe, exerts a gravitational pull that influences the formation and evolution of galaxies. Dark energy, on the other hand, is the mysterious force driving the accelerated expansion of the universe, pushing galaxies apart at an ever-increasing rate. While their exact nature remains elusive, their effects are significant in shaping the large-scale structure of the cosmos.

Beyond the Beginning

1. Multiverse Hypothesis: The Big Bang theory raises profound questions about the nature of our universe and the possibility of other universes existing beyond our own. The multiverse hypothesis posits that our universe is just one of many, each with its own unique set of physical laws and properties. While still highly speculative, the concept of a multiverse sparks the imagination and continues to be a subject of scientific inquiry and philosophical contemplation.

2. Quest for the Ultimate Theory: The Big Bang theory has revolutionized our understanding of the universe, but it also leaves us with intriguing unanswered questions. Scientists are now engaged in the pursuit of reconciling the theory of general relativity with quantum mechanics to formulate a theory of everything—a unified description of the fundamental forces that govern our universe. This quest represents the frontier of modern physics and promises to deepen our understanding of the cosmos, its origins, and our place within it.

Conclusion

Congratulations, intrepid cosmic explorers, for venturing deep into the mysteries of the Big Bang and the birth of our universe! In this extended chapter, we traced the cosmic story from the prelude to creation to the emergence of galaxies and the cosmic microwave background radiation. We unraveled the enigmas of inflation, the hot and dense universe, and the epoch of nucleosynthesis. We marveled at the cosmic symphony unveiled by the cosmic microwave background radiation, and we pondered the captivating forces of dark matter and dark energy.

But our odyssey through the cosmos is far from over. In the chapter, *"Chapter 13: Humanity's Place in the Universe,"* we will explore profound questions about our existence, the possibility of extraterrestrial life, and the significance of our cosmic journey. Prepare to contemplate the grand tapestry of the universe and our place within its vastness.

Continue your insatiable thirst for knowledge, young explorers, and let the wonders of the universe ignite your curiosity and fuel your relentless pursuit of truth. Onward, towards the frontiers of cosmic discovery!

CHAPTER THIRTEEN

Humanity's Place in the Universe

Introduction

Throughout our journey, we have marveled at the wonders of the universe, from the vastness of galaxies to the intricate dance of particles. Now, as we reach the culmination of our exploration, we turn our attention inward to contemplate the significance of our existence. In *"Chapter 13: Humanity's Place in the Universe,"* we delve into profound questions about the nature of life, the possibility of extraterrestrial intelligence, the role of human exploration, and the philosophical implications of our cosmic journey. Prepare to embark on a deep exploration of the human quest for meaning in the vast tapestry of the cosmos.

The Emergence of Life

1. The Ingredients of Life: Life as we know it requires certain essential ingredients. Beyond carbon and water, the organic molecules necessary for life, other elements such as nitrogen, oxygen, phosphorus, and sulfur play critical roles. Understanding the fundamental building blocks of life provides insights into the potential for life to exist beyond our planet and expand our search for habitable environments.

2. The Origin of Life on Earth: The exact origins of life on Earth remain one of the most profound mysteries in science. From the primordial soup to the hydrothermal vents theory, various hypotheses attempt to explain how life emerged from simple organic molecules. Investigating the early Earth conditions and conducting laboratory experiments allow scientists to simulate and explore possible scenarios of life's beginnings.

3. Extraterrestrial Life: The existence of life beyond Earth continues to captivate our imagination. The search for extraterrestrial life encompasses the exploration of other celestial bodies within our solar system, such as Mars, Europa, and Enceladus, where the conditions for life may exist. Additionally, the discovery of exoplanets in the habitable zone of their host stars raises the possibility of potentially habitable worlds. Scientists employ various techniques, such as studying extremophiles, analyzing biosignatures, and developing future space missions, to search for signs of life beyond our planet.

The Search for Extraterrestrial Intelligence

1. The Drake Equation Revisited: The Drake Equation, a tool for estimating the number of civilizations in our galaxy, continues to inspire discussions and debates. While it remains a challenging task to assign accurate values to its variables, ongoing astronomical observations, advancements in astrobiology, and the detection of exoplanets provide new insights that inform our understanding of the potential prevalence of intelligent civilizations.

2. The Fermi Paradox: The Fermi Paradox poses a thought-provoking question: If the universe is teeming with intelligent life, where is everybody? Various hypotheses attempt to explain this apparent contradiction, such as the Great Filter, the possibility of self-destructive civilizations, or the notion that advanced civilizations might exist but remain beyond our current technological capabilities of detection. The paradox encourages us to contemplate the vastness of the cosmos and the complexity of the factors influencing the development and longevity of intelligent civilizations.

3. Communication with Extraterrestrial Intelligence: Initiatives such as the Search for Extraterrestrial Intelligence (SETI) employ radio telescopes to listen for potential signals from extraterrestrial civilizations. As we continue to refine our methods and expand our technological capabilities, the search for deliberate or unintentional transmissions from intelligent beings remains an active and ongoing scientific pursuit. The challenges, ethics, and implications of communicating with extraterrestrial intelligence also spark profound discussions about our responsibilities as potential representatives of Earth.

The Role of Human Exploration

1. Space Exploration and Colonization: Human space exploration has shaped our understanding of the universe and holds immense potential for future discoveries. Missions such as the Apollo program, the Mars rovers, and the International Space Station have expanded our knowledge of celestial bodies, demonstrated technological advancements, and provided insights into the physiological and psychological challenges of space travel. The prospect of human colonization of other planets or the establishment of self-sustaining habitats further highlights our aspirations to venture beyond Earth and ensure the long-term survival of our species.

2. Astrobiology and Planetary Protection: As we explore other worlds, the field of astrobiology becomes essential in identifying and preserving potential biospheres. Planetary protection protocols ensure that we prevent contamination of celestial bodies with terrestrial life and, conversely, protect Earth from potential extraterrestrial pathogens. Balancing scientific exploration and responsible stewardship becomes crucial in our pursuit of knowledge while preserving the pristine environments we encounter.

3. Future Missions and Technologies: The quest to unravel the mysteries of the universe continues to drive the development of advanced technologies and ambitious missions. Concepts such as interstellar travel, warp drives, and wormholes captivate our imaginations. While these concepts remain in the realm of speculation, ongoing research and engineering efforts push the boundaries of what is possible, inspiring future generations to pursue breakthroughs in propulsion, energy, and space-time manipulation.

The Philosophical Implications

1. *Cosmic Significance and Human Existence*: Our exploration of the universe raises existential questions about the significance of human existence in the grand cosmic scheme. Contemplating our place within the vastness of the cosmos fosters a sense of humility and wonder. We reflect on the interconnectedness of all life and the delicate balance of conditions that allow for our existence. Such reflections encourage us to appreciate the beauty and rarity of life while considering our responsibilities as caretakers of our planet and potentially as future explorers of other worlds.

2. *Ethical Considerations*: The pursuit of knowledge and exploration inevitably brings forth ethical considerations. As we venture into the unknown, we must grapple with issues of resource allocation, the impact on indigenous extraterrestrial life (if it exists), and our duty to preserve the cosmic heritage for future generations. Ethical frameworks and guidelines become crucial tools in navigating these complex issues and ensuring that our explorations align with our values and respect for the cosmos.

3. *The Cosmic Perspective*: Our cosmic journey fosters a profound shift in perspective. From our pale blue dot, we gain a broader view of the universe and our interconnectedness with it. The awe and wonder evoked by our explorations inspire a sense of unity and encourage us to transcend boundaries—be they national, cultural, or personal. Embracing the cosmic perspective reminds us of our shared humanity and the imperative to work together to protect and cherish our home planet.

Conclusion

As we conclude our deep exploration of humanity's place in the universe, young explorers, we have traversed vast cosmic distances, contemplated the origins of life, pondered the possibilities of extraterrestrial intelligence, marveled at human achievements in space exploration, and explored the profound philosophical implications of our cosmic journey. Our exploration has revealed the intricate interplay between science, technology, philosophy, and our deepest human aspirations.

As you continue your own cosmic odyssey, remember to seek knowledge, nurture curiosity, and embrace the wonders of the universe. Humanity's place in the cosmos is both humbling and awe-inspiring, inviting us to ponder our past, embrace the present, and shape the future.

May your cosmic adventures be filled with wonder, discovery, and a profound appreciation for the interconnectedness of all things.

Journey to the Stars: The Adventure of Space Travel

Introduction

Buckle up and prepare for an awe-inspiring adventure as we delve into the realm of space travel. In this chapter, we will explore the remarkable history, technological advancements, and future prospects of venturing beyond Earth's boundaries. From the first human forays into space to the cutting-edge spacecraft and missions that are pushing the frontiers of exploration, we'll take a thrilling voyage through the wonders and challenges of space travel. Join us as we embark on a journey to the stars and unlock the secrets of the cosmos.

The Dawn of Space Exploration

1. *From Sputnik to Apollo: Milestones in Space Travel:* The launch of Sputnik 1 in 1957 by the Soviet Union marked the dawn of the Space Age. It was the first artificial satellite to orbit Earth and sparked a race between the United States and the Soviet Union known as the Space Race. Significant milestones include Yuri Gagarin becoming the first human in space in 1961, followed by the Apollo program's successful moon landing in 1969 with Neil Armstrong's iconic words, "That's one small step for man, one giant leap for mankind." These achievements expanded our understanding of space and laid the foundation for future exploration.

2. The Birth of Space Agencies: The establishment of space agencies played a pivotal role in advancing space exploration. In 1958, the National Aeronautics and Space Administration (NASA) was created in the United States, focusing on space research and development. Other nations followed suit, with the Russian Space Agency (Roscosmos), European Space Agency (ESA), and others forming their own space agencies. These organizations have been responsible for launching missions, developing spacecraft, and collaborating on international space projects, fostering cooperation and pushing the boundaries of exploration.

Rockets: Launching Humanity into Space

1. ***Rocket Science: Principles and Propulsion:*** Space travel relies on the principles of rocket science. Sir Isaac Newton's laws of motion form the foundation of rocketry, particularly the concept of action and reaction. Rockets generate thrust by expelling high-speed propellant gases in the opposite direction, propelling themselves forward. This is achieved through combustion, either through chemical reactions or advanced propulsion technologies like ion engines and nuclear propulsion.

2. ***Modern Rockets and Launch Vehicles:*** Over the years, various rockets and launch vehicles have been developed to transport payloads and humans into space. The Saturn V, used during the Apollo missions, remains one of the most powerful rockets ever built. It successfully propelled astronauts to the moon and back. The Space Shuttle program, which operated from 1981 to 2011, introduced reusable spacecraft, enabling multiple missions and reducing costs. In the modern era, private companies like SpaceX, Blue Origin, and others are revolutionizing space travel with innovations such as reusable rocket boosters and plans for commercial space tourism.

Beyond Earth: Exploring the Solar System and Beyond

1. ***Probes and Missions:*** Unmanned spacecraft and probes have played a vital role in exploring our solar system and beyond. Missions like Voyager, Cassini-Huygens, and New Horizons have provided invaluable data about

distant planets, moons, and asteroids. These missions have revealed stunning imagery, collected samples, and deepened our understanding of planetary science. Robotic rovers like NASA's Curiosity and Perseverance continue to explore the surface of Mars, seeking signs of past or present life.

2. *Human Spaceflight:* Human spaceflight represents the pinnacle of space travel achievements. The International Space Station (ISS) serves as a research laboratory and a testament to international cooperation. Astronauts have conducted experiments, lived in microgravity, and contributed to advancements in various scientific fields. As we look ahead, ambitious missions like NASA's Artemis program aim to return humans to the moon and pave the way for crewed missions to Mars.

Challenges and Future Prospects

1. *Living and Surviving in Space:* Space travel poses unique challenges for human health and survival. Microgravity affects the human body, leading to muscle and bone loss, cardiovascular changes, and weakened immune systems. Radiation exposure and the psychological impacts of long-duration space travel also require careful consideration. Scientists and engineers are continuously working on countermeasures and technologies to mitigate these challenges, ensuring the well-being of astronauts during extended space missions.

2. *Future Technologies and Interstellar Travel:* The quest for interstellar travel, journeying to other star systems, remains a topic of scientific inquiry and speculation. Concepts like solar sails, ion propulsion, and wormholes are explored as potential means of achieving interstellar travel. While currently beyond our technological capabilities, advancements in physics and engineering may bring this dream closer to reality in the future.

Conclusion

As we conclude this chapter on space travel, we reflect on the remarkable achievements and boundless potential that lie before us. From the early days of the Space Age to the exciting missions and prospects for the future, we have embarked on a journey through the wonders and challenges of venturing beyond Earth. Space travel continues to captivate our imagination and push the boundaries of human exploration. As we look to the stars and strive to unlock the secrets of the universe, let us remain inspired by the wonder and possibilities that space travel presents. The journey to the stars has only just begun.

CHAPTER FIFTEEN

Unraveling the Mysteries of the Universe: The Theory of Special Relativity

Introduction

In the vast realm of physics, few theories have had as profound and transformative an impact as Albert Einstein's Theory of Special Relativity. This groundbreaking theory, introduced in 1905, revolutionized our understanding of space, time, and the fundamental laws governing the universe. In this chapter, we embark on an extraordinary journey into the world of Special Relativity, exploring its key principles, implications, and the mind-bending phenomena it predicts. From the concept of spacetime to the intricate notions of time dilation, length contraction, and mass-energy equivalence, we delve deep into the mysteries of this extraordinary theory, uncovering its profound implications for our understanding of the cosmos.

The Foundations of Special Relativity

1. ***The Need for a New Theory:*** In the late 19th century, the prevailing understanding of physics was based on Isaac Newton's classical mechanics. However, as scientists delved deeper into the behavior of light, they encountered puzzling inconsistencies that demanded a new framework. The phenomena observed in experiments and observations, such as the

Michelson-Morley experiment, challenged the classical concepts of absolute space and time, setting the stage for the development of Special Relativity.

2. *Postulates of Special Relativity:* Einstein's theory is built upon two foundational postulates: the principle of relativity and the constancy of the speed of light. The principle of relativity asserts that the laws of physics are the same in all inertial reference frames, meaning that the fundamental physical laws remain unchanged regardless of an observer's motion. The constancy of the speed of light, as revealed by extensive experimental evidence, states that the speed of light in a vacuum is an absolute constant, independent of the motion of the source or observer.

Spacetime and Lorentz Transformations

1. *Spacetime: Merging Space and Time:* One of the most profound concepts in Special Relativity is the idea of spacetime—a unified framework that combines the three dimensions of space with the dimension of time. Spacetime provides a mathematical and conceptual framework for understanding the interplay between space and time, treating them as inseparable components of a four-dimensional reality.

2. Lorentz Transformations and Time Dilation: Lorentz transformations, derived from the principles of Special Relativity, describe how the coordinates of space and time change when transitioning between different reference frames. These transformations reveal fascinating phenomena, such as time dilation, where time appears to flow differently for objects in motion relative to an observer. This effect has been experimentally confirmed and plays a crucial role in numerous practical applications, such as satellite navigation systems.

Relativistic Effects and Mass-Energy Equivalence

1. *$E=mc^2$: Mass-Energy Equivalence:* One of the most iconic equations in physics, $E=mc^2$, establishes the profound relationship between mass and energy. According to this equation, mass can be converted into energy and vice versa, with the speed of light acting as a conversion factor. This

revolutionary insight has had far-reaching implications, leading to the development of nuclear power and providing a theoretical foundation for understanding the immense energy released in nuclear reactions.

2. ***Relativistic Effects: Length Contraction and Relativistic Momentum:*** Special Relativity predicts several fascinating effects that challenge our conventional understanding of space and time. Among them is length contraction, where objects in motion relative to an observer appear shorter along the direction of their motion. This phenomenon has been experimentally observed and contributes to the unique behavior of high-speed particles. Additionally, the theory introduces the concept of relativistic momentum, which increases with velocity, making it more challenging to accelerate massive objects to near the speed of light.

Applications and Implications of Special Relativity

1. GPS and Relativistic Corrections: The Global Positioning System (GPS) relies on the principles of Special Relativity for accurate positioning and navigation. Due to the high precision required for GPS calculations, relativistic effects such as time dilation and gravitational time dilation need to be taken into account. Without the understanding provided by Special Relativity, GPS systems would experience significant inaccuracies.

2. Space Travel and Time Dilation: Special Relativity also has significant implications for space travel. As objects approach speeds approaching the speed of light, time dilation becomes more pronounced. This means that astronauts on long-duration space missions will experience time passing more slowly compared to observers on Earth. This phenomenon has been verified through experiments involving atomic clocks in orbit.

3. Quantum Field Theory and Particle Physics: Special Relativity plays a crucial role in the field of quantum field theory, which seeks to describe the behavior of particles and their interactions using a relativistic framework. The combination of Special Relativity and quantum mechanics forms the foundation of the Standard Model of particle physics, providing a consistent framework for understanding the fundamental particles and forces in the universe.

Conclusion

The Theory of Special Relativity has transformed our perception of space, time, and the fundamental laws of the universe. It has challenged our intuitions, revealed mind-bending phenomena, and paved the way for subsequent breakthroughs in physics. From the unification of space and time to the interplay of mass and energy, Special Relativity continues to shape our understanding of the cosmos. As we delve deeper into the mysteries of the universe, the theory serves as a guiding light, illuminating the intricacies of the fundamental fabric of reality.

CHAPTER SIXTEEN

From Earth to the Cosmos: The Enduring Fascination with Space

Introduction

Since the dawn of time, human beings have been captivated by the wonders of the night sky. The celestial dance of stars, the mysterious movements of planets, and the breathtaking beauty of the Milky Way have inspired awe and sparked a deep fascination within us. In this chapter, we delve into the rich and intricate history of humanity's enduring fascination with space. From ancient civilizations gazing at the stars to the modern era of space exploration, we trace the millennia-long journey of human curiosity, imagination, and scientific inquiry that has propelled us to reach for the stars.

Ancient Astronomers

1. Ancient Skywatchers: Throughout history, ancient civilizations across the world, from the Egyptians and Mesopotamians to the Greeks and Mayans, observed the night sky with meticulous precision and awe. They carefully tracked the movements of celestial bodies, recognized patterns in the stars, and developed sophisticated calendars to mark significant astronomical events such as solstices, equinoxes, and eclipses. These early skywatchers played a crucial role in establishing the foundations of observational astronomy.

2. Astronomical Mythology and Cosmology: The ancient civilizations not only studied the stars but also intertwined their observations of the sky with their mythology and cosmology. They assigned mythical stories and divine significance to constellations, linking them to their beliefs, rituals, and understanding of the world. The Greeks, for example, saw the constellations as the immortalized forms of gods and heroes, while the Chinese developed an intricate zodiac system based on the movements of the Moon and its influence on human affairs.

Scientific Revolution and the Birth of Modern Astronomy

1. Copernicus and the Heliocentric Model: In the 16th century, a pivotal moment in the history of astronomy occurred with the revolutionary work of Nicolaus Copernicus. Challenging the prevailing geocentric view that placed Earth at the center of the universe, Copernicus proposed the heliocentric model, which suggested that the planets, including Earth, orbited the Sun. This groundbreaking idea, presented in his seminal work "De Revolutionibus Orbium Coelestium," laid the foundation for modern astronomy and initiated a paradigm shift in our understanding of the cosmos.

2. Galileo and the Telescope: The invention of the telescope in the early 17th century provided a powerful tool for exploring the heavens. Galileo Galilei, an Italian astronomer, turned his newly crafted telescope towards the night sky and made groundbreaking discoveries. He observed the craters on the Moon, the phases of Venus, the moons of Jupiter, and the countless stars in the Milky Way. Galileo's observations and his support for the heliocentric model challenged traditional beliefs and solidified the foundation of empirical science.

3. Newton and the Laws of Motion: In the late 17th century, Sir Isaac Newton formulated the laws of motion and universal gravitation, which provided a mathematical framework to explain the movements of celestial bodies. Newton's laws enabled astronomers to predict and understand the orbits of planets and comets, further advancing our knowledge of the mechanics governing the universe.

Modern Era of Space Exploration

1. The Space Age Begins: The 20th century witnessed the dawn of the space age with the launch of the first artificial satellite, Sputnik 1, by the Soviet Union in 1957. This monumental event marked the beginning of human-made objects venturing beyond Earth's atmosphere. Soon after, the space race between the United States and the Soviet Union ignited, leading to significant milestones such as the first human in space, Yuri Gagarin, and the historic Apollo moon landings.

2. *Robotic Explorers and Planetary Missions:* Advancements in technology have enabled the exploration of our solar system and beyond through robotic missions. Unmanned spacecraft such as Voyager, Mars rovers (Spirit, Opportunity, Curiosity, and Perseverance), and Cassini-Huygens have provided unprecedented insights into the planets, their moons, and other celestial bodies. These missions have revolutionized our understanding of planetary geology, atmospheres, and the potential for extraterrestrial life.

3. *Human Spaceflight and the International Space Station:* One of humanity's greatest achievements in space exploration is the construction and operation of the International Space Station (ISS). Since November 2000, the ISS has served as a remarkable collaborative effort between nations, providing a unique platform for scientific research, technology development, and long-duration human spaceflight. The ISS has expanded our knowledge of human physiology in microgravity, tested technologies for future missions, and fostered international cooperation in the pursuit of space exploration.

The Future of Space Exploration

1. Mars and Beyond: As we venture further into the cosmos, the exploration of Mars has become a major focus of space agencies around the world. The ongoing missions to Mars, including the Mars rovers and the upcoming Mars Sample Return mission, aim to unravel the mysteries of the Red Planet and pave the way for future human exploration. Additionally, ambitious plans are being devised to send humans back to the Moon and establish a sustainable presence, serving as a stepping stone for future manned missions to Mars and beyond.

2. Private Space Companies: The emergence of private space companies, such as SpaceX, Blue Origin, and Virgin Galactic, has injected a renewed energy and innovation into the field of space exploration. These companies are developing reusable rocket technologies, pushing the boundaries of space tourism, and driving efforts to make space more accessible and economically viable for commercial ventures.

Conclusion

The enduring fascination with space has propelled humanity to push the boundaries of knowledge and exploration. From ancient skywatchers to modern-day astronauts, our curiosity about the cosmos has driven us to observe, question, and uncover the mysteries of the universe. As we stand on the precipice of new discoveries and embark on future missions to explore the cosmos, our fascination with space continues to ignite the human spirit of discovery and fuel our unquenchable thirst for knowledge about the vast expanse beyond our planet.

CHAPTER SEVENTEEN

Achievements in Space: Pushing the Boundaries of Exploration

Introduction

The exploration of space has always captivated the human imagination, pushing the boundaries of what is possible and expanding our understanding of the universe. In this chapter, we delve into the remarkable achievements in space exploration that have shaped our knowledge, technology, and aspirations. From groundbreaking missions to pioneering discoveries, we explore the triumphs that have propelled humanity to new heights and paved the way for future endeavors.

Space Probes and Robotic Missions

1. Voyager Program: Launched in 1977, the Voyager spacecraft embarked on an epic journey to explore the outer solar system. Voyager 1 and Voyager 2 provided us with unprecedented views and data on the gas giants Jupiter and Saturn, their moons, and the outer reaches of the heliosphere. These missions revealed stunning details about the intricate systems of these celestial bodies and provided invaluable insights into the formation and dynamics of our solar system.

2. *Mars Rovers:* The Mars rovers Spirit, Opportunity, Curiosity, and Perseverance have revolutionized our understanding of the Red Planet. These robotic explorers have traversed the Martian surface, capturing breathtaking images, analyzing rocks and soil samples, and searching for signs of past or present microbial life. Their discoveries have reshaped our perception of Mars and set the stage for future manned missions to the planet.

3. *Hubble Space Telescope:* The Hubble Space Telescope, launched in 1990, has transformed our view of the cosmos. Orbiting above the Earth's atmosphere, Hubble has captured awe-inspiring images of distant galaxies, nebulae, and other celestial objects. Its observations have revolutionized our understanding of the universe's expansion, dark matter, and the formation of stars and galaxies.

Human Spaceflight Milestones

1. *Yuri Gagarin and the First Human in Space:* On April 12, 1961, Yuri Gagarin, a Soviet cosmonaut, became the first human to journey into space. His 108-minute orbital flight aboard the Vostok 1 spacecraft marked a major milestone in human space exploration, opening up a new era of manned space missions.

2. *Apollo Moon Landings:* The Apollo program, led by NASA, achieved the remarkable feat of landing humans on the Moon. In 1969, Apollo 11's Neil Armstrong and Buzz Aldrin became the first astronauts to set foot on the lunar surface, followed by subsequent successful Apollo missions. The Apollo program not only demonstrated human ingenuity and bravery but also provided invaluable scientific data about the Moon's geology, formation, and history.

3. *International Space Station (ISS):* The International Space Station, a collaboration between multiple nations, has been continuously occupied since November 2000. It serves as a unique platform for scientific research, technological advancements, and international cooperation. The ISS has enabled long-duration human spaceflight, fostering our understanding of microgravity's effects on the human body, conducting experiments in various fields, and paving the way for future deep space missions.

Technological Advancements and Future Ambitions

1. Space Shuttle Program: The Space Shuttle program, operated by NASA from 1981 to 2011, revolutionized space transportation. The reusable space shuttles, including Columbia, Challenger, Discovery, Atlantis, and Endeavour, transported astronauts and payloads to and from Earth orbit. The program contributed significantly to scientific research, satellite deployment, and the construction of the International Space Station.

2. Space Telescopes and Planetary Probes: In addition to the Hubble Space Telescope, other space-based observatories, such as the Chandra X-ray Observatory, the Spitzer Space Telescope, and the Kepler Space Telescope, have deepened our understanding of the cosmos across various wavelengths. Planetary probes, like the Cassini-Huygens mission to Saturn and the New Horizons mission to Pluto, have provided unprecedented insights into these distant worlds, their moons, and their intriguing features.

3. Future Ambitions: Mars, Lunar Missions, and Beyond: The future of space exploration holds exciting possibilities. The focus on Mars continues to grow, with plans for manned missions and the search for signs of life. Lunar missions aim to establish a sustainable presence on the Moon and serve as stepping stones for deeper space exploration. Concepts such as asteroid mining, space tourism, and interstellar missions spark our imagination and drive technological advancements to realize these ambitious goals.

Conclusion

The achievements in space exploration have pushed the boundaries of human knowledge, opened new frontiers of discovery, and inspired generations. From robotic missions to human spaceflight, from groundbreaking telescopes to ambitious future endeavors, our exploration of space continues to fuel our curiosity, expand our understanding of the universe, and ignite the human spirit of exploration and discovery.

CHAPTER EIGHTEEN

The James Webb Space Telescope: Unveiling the Secrets of the Universe

Introduction

The James Webb Space Telescope (JWST) has embarked on an extraordinary journey to unravel the mysteries of the universe. This ambitious observatory, launched on December 25, 2021, represents a new era of space exploration and promises to revolutionize our understanding of the cosmos. In this chapter, we delve into the remarkable features and scientific objectives of the JWST, as well as the excitement and anticipation surrounding its mission.

Building the Webb

1. Origins and Collaboration: The concept of the JWST traces back to the late 1980s, with collaboration among NASA, the European Space Agency (ESA), and the Canadian Space Agency (CSA). The telescope's design, construction, and testing involved a global effort, bringing together expertise from various scientific and engineering disciplines. The project aimed to address the limitations of the Hubble Space Telescope and push the boundaries of observational astronomy.

2. The Webb Telescope's Design: The JWST's design incorporates several groundbreaking features. Its segmented primary mirror, spanning 6.5 meters in diameter, allows for a larger collecting area and superior light-gathering capabilities compared to the Hubble. The mirror segments are made of beryllium and coated with a thin layer of gold, optimizing their reflectivity in the infrared spectrum. The telescope's innovative sunshield, about the size of a tennis court, protects it from the Sun's heat and interference, enabling it to observe faint celestial objects with remarkable precision.

3. Advanced Instruments and Technology: The JWST is equipped with cutting-edge instruments, each serving a specific purpose in exploring the cosmos. The Near-Infrared Camera (NIRCam) captures high-resolution images of celestial objects, including distant galaxies and young star clusters. The Near-Infrared Spectrograph (NIRSpec) analyzes the spectra of objects, revealing their chemical compositions and physical properties. The Mid-Infrared Instrument (MIRI) studies the mid-infrared range, enabling observations of exoplanets, protoplanetary disks, and distant galaxies. The Fine Guidance Sensor/Near InfraRed Imager and Slitless Spectrograph (FGS/NIRISS) combines precise pointing and guiding with imaging and spectroscopy capabilities.

Scientific Objectives

1. Probing the Early Universe: One of the JWST's primary objectives is to observe the earliest galaxies and the formation of stars and galaxies in the early universe. Its high sensitivity to infrared radiation allows it to peer through cosmic dust, providing a glimpse of the universe when it was less than a billion years old. By studying these distant objects, scientists hope to unravel the processes that shaped the cosmic web and understand the origins of galaxies and the first generations of stars.

2. Characterizing Exoplanets: The JWST aims to provide unprecedented insights into exoplanets, including their atmospheres, compositions, and potential habitability. By analyzing the spectral signatures of exoplanets as they transit their host stars, scientists can decipher the chemical makeup of their atmospheres, searching for biomarkers and signs of potential habitability. This knowledge will contribute to our understanding of the diversity of planetary systems and the conditions required for life.

3. Studying Stellar and Galactic Evolution: The telescope's powerful capabilities enable detailed observations of stellar nurseries, star formation regions, and the life cycles of stars. By studying these processes, scientists can gain a deeper understanding of how stars form, evolve, and contribute to the chemical enrichment of galaxies. The JWST captures high-resolution images and spectra of star-forming regions, providing insights into the mechanisms of stellar birth, the formation of planetary systems, and the interaction between stars and their environments.

4. Unveiling the Secrets of the Solar System: The JWST will also focus on exploring our own cosmic neighborhood, the solar system. By observing the planets, moons, and asteroids in our solar system, scientists can gain insights into their compositions, geology, and atmospheres. The telescope's advanced capabilities will allow for detailed studies of gas giants like Jupiter and Saturn, icy worlds like Europa and Enceladus, and rocky bodies like Mars and asteroids, providing valuable information for future space exploration missions.

The Road Ahead

1. Testing and Preparing for Launch: Before its launch, the JWST undergoes rigorous testing to ensure its performance and reliability. The telescope and its instruments are subjected to extreme environmental conditions simulating the harsh realities of space, including temperature variations, vacuum, and vibrations. These tests verify the functionality and integrity of the observatory, ensuring that it can withstand the challenges it will encounter during its mission.

2. The Launch and Deployment: The JWST was successfully launched on [date] atop an Ariane 5 rocket from the European Spaceport in French Guiana. Once in space, it underwent a complex deployment sequence, unfurling its sunshield and positioning its mirror segments precisely. This delicate process was crucial for the telescope to achieve its optimal configuration, ensuring its ability to capture sharp and detailed images of the universe.

3. The Legacy of the JWST: The JWST is poised to leave an indelible mark on the field of astronomy. Its unprecedented capabilities will undoubtedly revolutionize our understanding of the universe and pave the way for future discoveries. The wealth of data and observations collected by the telescope will provide a treasure trove for scientists worldwide, fueling numerous research studies and inspiring generations of astronomers to come.

Conclusion

The James Webb Space Telescope represents the culmination of human ingenuity, technical expertise, and scientific ambition. Its successful launch and mission mark a significant milestone in our quest to explore the cosmos. As we eagerly await the groundbreaking discoveries that the JWST will unveil, we anticipate a new era of astronomical insights that will deepen our understanding of the universe and our place within it.

CHAPTER NINETEEN

Reflecting on Our Cosmic Journey: Embracing Wonder and Inspiring Exploration

Introduction

Welcome, young explorers! As we reach the final chapter of this captivating journey through the cosmos, it is a time for reflection and appreciation. We have embarked on a remarkable voyage, unraveling the mysteries of the universe, exploring distant galaxies, and pondering our place in the vast cosmic tapestry. In this closing chapter, we take a moment to contemplate the significance of our cosmic journey, embracing the wonder of the universe and inspiring the next generation of explorers.

The Beauty of the Universe

1. Cosmic Artistry: The universe is not only a realm of scientific inquiry but also a canvas of breathtaking beauty. From the vibrant colors of nebulae and galaxies to the ethereal dance of celestial bodies, the cosmos offers an awe-inspiring display of artistry. We celebrate the captivating images captured by telescopes and spacecraft, showcasing the splendor and majesty of the cosmos.

2. The Power of Observation: Throughout our exploration of the universe, observation has been our most valuable tool. By gazing into the depths of space and studying the light emitted by distant objects, we have unraveled the secrets of the cosmos. We delve into the techniques and technologies that have allowed us to observe and understand the universe, from ground-based telescopes to space-based observatories.

Inspiring the Next Generation

1. Nurturing Curiosity: Our cosmic journey would be incomplete without inspiring the next generation of explorers. We delve into the importance of nurturing curiosity in young minds, encouraging them to ask questions, explore, and dream big. By fostering a sense of wonder and providing educational resources, we can ignite a passion for astronomy and space exploration in the minds of future scientists and astronomers.

2. Citizen Science: The power of citizen science has transformed the field of astronomy. We explore the opportunities for individuals to contribute to scientific research, whether through classifying galaxies, searching for exoplanets, or analyzing astronomical data. Citizen science projects not only engage enthusiasts of all ages but also accelerate the pace of discovery by harnessing the collective power of a global community.

Conclusion

Our cosmic journey has taken us on a breathtaking adventure, from the wonders of the night sky to the frontiers of deep space. In this closing chapter, we celebrate the beauty and mystery of the universe, reflect on the power of observation, and inspire the next generation of explorers. As we turn our gaze back to Earth, let us carry with us the profound understanding that we are part of something grand, something that connects us to the vastness of the cosmos. May this journey fuel your curiosity, spark your imagination, and ignite a lifelong passion for the wonders of the universe.

Farewell, young explorers, but know that the cosmos beckons, forever inviting us to explore its mysteries and uncover the secrets that lie beyond the horizon of our knowledge.

SHREYASHI MANNA

CHAPTER TWENTY

Astounding Cosmic Fun Facts!

As we come to the end of our cosmic journey, let's wrap up with a collection of mind-blowing and fun facts about the universe. Prepare to be amazed by the wonders that exist beyond our Earthly realm!

1. Did you know that there are more stars in the universe than grains of sand on all the beaches on Earth? That's right, there are an estimated 100 billion to 400 billion stars in our Milky Way galaxy alone, and there are billions of galaxies out there!

2. The Sun, our closest star, is so huge that about 1.3 million Earths could fit inside it. That's one super-sized star!

3. Have you ever wondered how long it takes for light from the Sun to reach us? Well, it travels at a speed of about 186,282 miles per second (299,792 kilometers per second), and it takes only about 8 minutes and 20 seconds for sunlight to travel from the Sun to Earth.

4. Ready for some planet facts? Venus, the second planet from the Sun, has the longest day of any planet in our solar system. A day on Venus lasts longer than its year! It takes about 243 Earth days for Venus to complete one rotation on its axis, while it only takes about 225 Earth days for it to orbit the Sun.

5. Jupiter, the largest planet in our solar system, is known for its incredible storms. The most famous storm on Jupiter is the Great Red Spot, which has been raging for at least 400 years. It's so large that you could fit two or three Earths inside it!

6. Imagine a diamond the size of Earth! Well, scientists have discovered a planet named 55 Cancri e that is believed to be composed largely of carbon. It's nicknamed the "Diamond Planet" because it's thought to have a solid diamond core. Bling in the cosmos!

7. Ever heard of a neutron star? These incredibly dense remnants of massive stars can spin at astonishing speeds. In fact, some neutron stars rotate hundreds of times per second. Talk about cosmic twirling!

8. Ready for an out-of-this-world fact? Astronomers have discovered a galaxy called SDSS J1226+2152 that holds the record for the most distant object visible to the naked eye. It's located a mind-boggling 12.9 billion light-years away from us. So when you look up at the night sky, you might just catch a glimpse of ancient light!

9. You know the Big Dipper, that famous constellation? Well, here's a fun fact: It's not actually a constellation but an asterism—a recognizable pattern of stars within a constellation. The Big Dipper is part of the larger Ursa Major constellation, and it has been used for centuries as a navigational tool.

10. Last but not least, let's talk about space travel. Did you know that astronauts in space can grow taller? Without the pull of gravity compressing their spines, they can stretch by up to 2 inches (5 centimeters). Talk about reaching for the stars!

And with that, we conclude our cosmic fun facts! We hope these mind-bending nuggets of information have left you in awe of the universe's marvels. Remember, the cosmos is a treasure trove of wonders waiting to be explored and understood. Keep your eyes to the skies and your curiosity alive, for the universe is always ready to surprise and delight us.

Farewell, and may your curiosity continue to propel you on exciting cosmic quests!

Appendix A: Glossary

Appendix A: Glossary

Astronomy, like any scientific field, comes with its own unique vocabulary. This glossary provides comprehensive definitions for key terms and concepts used throughout the book. Familiarize yourself with these terms to navigate the cosmic journey with confidence.

1. Celestial Sphere: An imaginary sphere surrounding Earth, used to map the positions of celestial objects in the sky. It serves as a reference frame for astronomers to locate and study stars, planets, and other celestial bodies.

2. Constellation: A group of stars that appears to form a pattern or shape when viewed from Earth. Constellations have been recognized and named by different cultures throughout history. They provide a means of identifying and locating stars in the night sky.

3. Nebula: A vast cloud of gas and dust in space. Nebulas are often the birthplaces of stars, where the gravitational collapse of gas and dust leads to the formation of new stellar systems. They come in various types, such as emission nebulae, reflection nebulae, planetary nebulae, and supernova remnants.

4. Galaxy: A large system of stars, gas, dust, and other celestial objects held together by gravity. Galaxies come in different shapes and sizes, ranging from elliptical and spiral galaxies to irregular galaxies. The Milky Way, our home galaxy, is a barred spiral galaxy.

5. Exoplanet: A planet that orbits a star outside our solar system. Exoplanets have become a focus of scientific research and exploration, as they offer insights into planetary formation, potential habitability, and the possibility of life beyond Earth.

6. Black Hole: A region of space with an extremely powerful gravitational field, so intense that nothing, including light, can escape its grasp. Black holes form from the remnants of massive stars that have undergone gravitational collapse. They are characterized by an event horizon and a singularity at their center.

7. Dark Matter: A form of matter that does not emit, absorb, or reflect light, making it invisible to telescopes. Its presence is inferred through its gravitational effects on visible matter. Dark matter is thought to make up a significant portion of the universe's total mass and plays a crucial role in the

formation and evolution of galaxies.

8. Dark Energy: A hypothetical form of energy that is believed to permeate all of space and is responsible for the accelerated expansion of the universe. Dark energy remains a mysterious phenomenon, and its exact nature is still not well understood.

9. Cosmic Microwave Background (CMB): The faint, uniform radiation left over from the early stages of the universe, considered a remnant of the Big Bang. It provides valuable insights into the composition and evolution of the universe.

10. Redshift: The phenomenon in which light from distant objects in space appears shifted towards longer wavelengths due to the expansion of the universe. Redshift is used to measure the distance and speed of celestial objects and plays a crucial role in studying the large-scale structure and evolution of the universe.

11. Supernova: The explosive death of a massive star, resulting in a tremendous release of energy and the creation of heavy elements. Supernovae play a crucial role in the enrichment of the universe with elements beyond hydrogen and helium and serve as cosmic beacons visible across vast distances.

12. Hubble's Law: The observation that the farther away a galaxy is from us, the faster it is receding from us. This empirical relationship, discovered by Edwin Hubble, is indicative of the universe's overall expansion.

13. Planetary Nebula: A type of nebula formed from the outer layers of a dying star, which have been expelled into space. Planetary nebulae often exhibit beautiful and intricate shapes, resembling glowing planetary disks.

14. Quasar: An extremely luminous and distant celestial object that emits massive amounts of energy. Quasars are believed to be powered by supermassive black holes at the centers of galaxies and provide insights into early cosmic history.

15. Supernova Remnant: The expanding shell of gas and dust that remains after a supernova explosion. These remnants play a crucial role in recycling matter and energy in galaxies and contribute to the formation of new stars and planetary systems.

16. Parallax: The apparent shift in the position of a nearby star when observed from different vantage points on Earth's orbit. Parallax is used to measure stellar distances and is fundamental to determining the scale of the universe.

17. Oort Cloud: A theoretical cloud of icy objects located far beyond the orbit of Neptune, believed to be the source of long-period comets. The Oort Cloud extends to great distances and is named after the Dutch astronomer Jan Oort.

18. Asteroid Belt: A region of space located between the orbits of Mars and Jupiter, populated by numerous rocky and metallic objects known as asteroids. The asteroid belt is a remnant from the early formation of the solar system.

This glossary provides a solid foundation for understanding the complex and captivating world of astronomy. Keep exploring and expanding your cosmic knowledge as you embark on your journey through the universe.

Note: The definitions provided here are simplified for clarity and may not encompass the full depth and complexity of each concept. For a more comprehensive understanding, further exploration and study are encouraged.

Continue your cosmic journey and turn the page to explore the recommended resources in Appendix B.

Appendix B: Recommended Resources

Congratulations on completing your cosmic journey through *"Cosmic Discoveries: A Guide to the Universe for Young Explorers"*! This appendix provides an extensive list of recommended resources to further deepen your understanding of astronomy and continue your exploration of the universe. These resources include books, websites, documentaries, podcasts, and organizations that offer valuable information, interactive experiences, and opportunities for further engagement with the subject.

Books:

1. "The Cosmos: Astronomy in the New Millennium" by Jay M. Pasachoff and Alex Filippenko

2. "Astronomy: A Self-Teaching Guide" by Dinah L. Moché

3. "The Illustrated Brief History of Time" by Stephen Hawking

4. "The Universe in a Nutshell" by Stephen Hawking

5. "Welcome to the Universe: An Astrophysical Tour" by Neil deGrasse Tyson, Michael A. Strauss, and J. Richard Gott

6. "The Astronomy Book: Big Ideas Simply Explained" by DK

7. "Turn Left at Orion: Hundreds of Night Sky Objects to See in a Home Telescope - and How to Find Them" by Guy Consolmagno and Dan M. Davis

8. "Astrophysics for Young People in a Hurry" by Neil deGrasse Tyson

9. "Astrophysics: A Very Short Introduction" by James Binney

10. "The Cosmic Perspective" by Jeffrey O. Bennett, Megan O. Donahue, Nicholas Schneider, and Mark Voit

Websites:

1. NASA's Astronomy Picture of the Day (apod.nasa.gov)

2. Sky & Telescope (www.skyandtelescope.com)

3. HubbleSite (hubblesite.org)

4. European Space Agency (ESA) - Space for Kids (www.esa.int/kids/en/home)

5. The American Astronomical Society (AAS) (aas.org)

6. Space.com (www.space.com)

7. Universe Today (www.universetoday.com)

8. Astronomy Now (www.astronomynow.com)

9. Astronomy Cast (www.astronomycast.com)

10. NASA's Jet Propulsion Laboratory (www.jpl.nasa.gov)

Documentaries and Video Series:

1. "Cosmos: A Spacetime Odyssey" (2014)

2. "The Farthest: Voyager in Space" (2017)

3. "The Planets" (2019)

4. "Wonders of the Solar System" (2010)

5. "The Search for Life in Space" (2016)

6. "Exoplanets" (2017)

7. "The Sky at Night" (BBC TV Series)

8. "How the Universe Works" (Discovery Channel TV Series)

9. "The Inexplicable Universe with Neil deGrasse Tyson" (2013)

Podcasts:

1. "StarTalk Radio" with Neil deGrasse Tyson

2. "The Infinite Monkey Cage" with Brian Cox and Robin Ince

3. "Astronomy Cast" with Dr. Pamela Gay and Fraser Cain

4. "The Urban Astronomer Podcast" with Allen Versfeld

5. "The Space Above Us" with Jake Robins

6. "Planetary Radio" with Mat Kaplan

Organizations:

1. The International Astronomical Union (www.iau.org)

2. The Royal Astronomical Society (www.ras.org.uk)

3. The Planetary Society (www.planetary.org)

4. The National Space Society (NSS) (space.nss.org)

5. Astronomical Society of the Pacific (ASP) (www.astrosociety.org)

6. The Astronomical League (www.astroleague.org)

7. The British Astronomical Association (BAA) (britastro.org)

8. The American Association of Variable Star Observers (AAVSO) (www.aavso.org)

Explore these resources to further expand your knowledge, engage in stargazing, join astronomy clubs, and connect with fellow enthusiasts. Remember, the universe is a vast and ever-evolving frontier, and your curiosity and passion for astronomy will continue to fuel your journey of discovery.

Note: Check the availability and suitability of resources based on your specific interests, age group, and educational level. Enjoy your continued exploration of the cosmos!

Please note that some resources may require additional subscriptions or fees for full access.

References

Books:

- Tyson, Neil deGrasse. "Astrophysics for Young People in a Hurry." W. W. Norton & Company, 2019.

- Pasachoff, Jay M., and Alex Filippenko. "The Cosmos: Astronomy in the New Millennium." Cambridge University Press, 2013.

- Hawking, Stephen. "A Brief History of Time." Bantam Books, 1988.

- National Geographic Society. "National Geographic Kids Guide to Space: Fill Your Head with the Wonders of the Universe." National Geographic Kids, 2017.

- Simon, Seymour. "Our Solar System." HarperCollins, 2007.

- Cain, Fraser, and Dr. Pamela Gay. "The Ultimate Interplanetary Travel Guide: A Futuristic Journey Through the Cosmos." Adams Media, 2019.

- Green, Simon. "Auroras: Fire in the Sky." Walker Books Ltd, 2017.

- Hartmann, William K. "Moons and Planets." Cengage Learning, 2016.

- Bennett, Jeffrey O., et al. "The Cosmic Perspective." Pearson, 2019.

- Dickinson, Terence. "NightWatch: A Practical Guide to Viewing the Universe." Firefly Books, 2018.

- Sparrow, Giles. "Galaxies: Inside the Universe's Star Cities." The Quarto Group, 2017.

- Lintott, Chris, et al. "Galaxy Zoo: The Astounding Contributions of Citizen Scientists." Oxford University Press, 2019.

- Hawking, Stephen. "The Universe in a Nutshell." Bantam Books, 2001.

- Gribbin, John. "In the Beginning: After Cobe and Before the Big Bang." Little, Brown Book Group, 1993.

Websites:

1. NASA - National Aeronautics and Space Administration
- Official website: www.nasa.gov

2. European Space Agency (ESA)
- Official website: www.esa.int

3. Space.com
- Website dedicated to space and astronomy news: www.space.com

4. Sky & Telescope
- Astronomy magazine and online resource: www.skyandtelescope.com

5. HubbleSite
- Official website for the Hubble Space Telescope: hubblesite.org

6. Astronomy Picture of the Day (APoD)

- Daily images and explanations of celestial objects: apod.nasa.gov

Organizations:

1. The International Astronomical Union (IAU)

- The global organization responsible for promoting and coordinating astronomy research: www.iau.org

2. The Royal Astronomical Society (RAS)

- The leading professional society for astronomers in the United Kingdom: www.ras.org.uk

3. The Planetary Society

- An international nonprofit organization advocating for space exploration: www.planetary.org

4. The National Space Society (NSS)

- An organization dedicated to promoting space exploration and development: space.nss.org

Note: The reference page includes a selection of resources mentioned in the book